TEACHING EARLY YEARS MATHEMATICS, SCIENCE AND ICT

Geoff Hilton
Annette Hilton
Shelley Dole
Chris Campbell

TEACHING EARLY YEARS MATHEMATICS, SCIENCE AND ICT

Core concepts and practice for the first three years of schooling

LONDON AND NEW YORK

First published 2014 by Allen & Unwin

Published 2020 by Routledge
2 Park Square, Milton Park, Abingdon, Oxon OX14 4RN
605 Third Avenue, New York, NY 10017

First issued in hardback 2021

Routledge is an imprint of the Taylor & Francis Group, an informa business

Copyright © Geoff Hilton, Annette Hilton, Shelley Dole and Chris Campbell 2014

All rights reserved. No part of this book may be reprinted or reproduced or utilised
in any form or by any electronic, mechanical, or other means, now known or
hereafter invented, including photocopying and recording, or in any information
storage or retrieval system, without permission in writing from the publishers.

Notice:
Product or corporate names may be trademarks or registered trademarks, and are
used only for identification and explanation without intent to infringe.

Publisher's Note
The publisher has gone to great lengths to ensure the quality of this reprint but
points out that some imperfections in the original copies may be apparent.

Cataloguing-in-Publication details are available
from the National Library of Australia
www.trove.nla.gov.au

Internal design by Simon Paterson, Bookhouse
Index by Puddingburn Publishing Services
Set in 11/14 pt Minion Pro by Bookhouse, Sydney

ISBN 13: 978-0-367-71959-3 (hbk)
ISBN 13: 978-1-74331-441-8 (pbk)

Contents

About the authors		vii
Introduction		ix
1	Teaching young children in the first three years of schooling	1
2	Information and communication technology in the first three years of schooling	9
3	Science in the first three years of schooling	25
4	Biological science	31
5	Chemical science	52
6	Earth and space science	70
7	Physical science	90
8	Making ICT integral to a science lesson sequence: Biology	110
9	Mathematics in the first three years of schooling	123
10	Number and Algebra	139
11	Statistics and Probability	173
12	Geometry and Measurement	180
13	Making ICT integral to mathematics: Time	197
A final note		209
References		211
Index		215

About the authors

Dr Geoff Hilton is a postdoctoral fellow in the School of Education at The University of Queensland. He currently lectures and coordinates numeracy courses for the Bachelor of Education and Masters of Teaching programs as well as a Teaching and Learning course for the Graduate Diploma programme. He was a primary school teacher for 28 years. Geoff's research interests include children's acquisition of numeracy concepts, links between mathematics and science, and in- and pre-service teacher education.

Dr Annette Hilton is an Associate Professor in Science Education at Aarhus University in Copenhagen, Denmark. She was a science and mathematics teacher for 20 years. She has worked as a lecturer in science education at Australian Catholic University and was a postdoctoral fellow at The University of Queensland, Australia. Annette has lectured in science and mathematics education as well as learning theory and action research courses within Bachelor of Education, Graduate Diploma of Education and Masters of Teaching programs. Over the past six years Annette and Geoff have presented teacher professional development workshops on numeracy, digital technologies and science education in Australia, UAE, Tanzania and Denmark. Annette's research interests include conceptual and representational competence development in school science and mathematics, interconnections between mathematics and science and in- and pre-service teacher development.

Dr Shelley Dole is an Associate Professor in the School of Education at The University of Queensland, where she coordinates Mathematics Curriculum Studies for prospective primary and middle school teachers in the pre-service Bachelor of Education program. Over the 20 years she has been in education, she has taught in primary, secondary and tertiary teaching institutions throughout Australia. Her research interests includ mathematics curriculum change and innovation; learning difficulties, misconceptions and conceptual change associated with learning mathematics; and particularly rational number topics of ratio and per cent and the development of proportional reasoning and multiplicative structures. She has led two major Australian Research Council projects focusing on numeracy across the curriculum and the development of proportional reasoning, with teachers and schools in Queensland and South Australia. She has been involved in several major research projects in Queensland, Tasmania, Victoria and South Australia including middle years literacy and numeracy; early years literacy and numeracy and distance education; mental computation, number sense and invented algorithms; teaching and learning per cent in the middle school; basic facts in the early years, as well as teacher professional development projects.

Dr Chris Campbell is a Lecturer in ICT Education in the School of Education at The University of Queensland. Chris, a primary school teacher, began teaching in NSW before beginning a lecturing career at La Trobe University in 2005 where she worked for over 4 years. She has since worked at The University of Notre Dame Australia, prior to beginning at The University of Queensland in 2010. Her research interests include the use of technology in the classroom as well as for teaching. Chris was chief investigator of an Australian Research Council (ARD) grant that explored 'Pedagogical approaches that influence students' learning and capacity for self-regulation'.

Introduction

This text is intended for use by pre-service and in-service teachers of children who are in the first three years of schooling. These children typically range in age from 5 to 8 years. The focus is on teaching science and mathematics, and the integration of information and communication technology (ICT). Each of these three areas is presented in separate chapters to ensure that the development of concepts and skills is addressed adequately; however, the intention is *not* for teachers to consider them as discrete areas. Indeed, it is important that teachers make as many connections as possible among the areas of learning. Suggestions for integration across subjects are provided throughout the book, but we encourage readers to develop their own ideas and strategies for making connections.

Teaching and learning in the first three years of schooling can be very complex. Teachers with many years of experience will say that they never stop learning about their chosen profession. We feel that addressing all aspects of this complexity would be counter-productive. Therefore, while including some aspects of teaching and learning theory, we have kept the focus on the practical aspects and examples of teaching science, mathematics and ICT in the first three years of schooling.

The text is designed to present some ways of teaching the big ideas and important concepts that exist in the areas of science, mathematics and ICT. These ideas are common to curricula across countries, and it is our intention to have the active reader seek and make specific links among the ideas presented and the relevant curriculum. In addition, the balance of theory and practice in this text is deliberate. We see it as a text that exists alongside others that deal specifically with the separate subject areas. Our intention is to more closely replicate the integration that occurs in classrooms by presenting practical teaching ideas and making specific links among the three areas of science, mathematics and ICT. Each of the curriculum sections of this book begins with an overview to help align the reader's thinking with the authors' intentions.

Specific year levels are not assigned to the examples given in this text, as early schooling content may vary from country to country and context to context. However, the learning episodes provide flexibility for the teacher to use judgement as to what is suitable for a particular year level or cohort. For example, the structure and enactment of learning sequences may differ considerably depending on children's reading and writing ability or available classroom resources.

Because teachers (particularly in the early school years) must be flexible, creative and responsive to their students' needs and abilities, this text does not set out to be overly prescriptive. The teaching and learning episodes are intended as illustrations of possibilities, to be used as thinking springboards, to be reconfigured and to be developed to more specifically meet teachers' needs and those of their young students. Having said this, while the mathematics section is quite content prescriptive, the methods of facilitating the children's learning of this content can be very flexible. In addition, many of the approaches used throughout the book can be adapted for use across all curriculum areas.

Overview of this book

Chapter 1 sets the scene for the rest of the book. It foregrounds important aspects of teaching that are relevant to mathematics, science and ICT in the first three years of schooling. It gives a brief insight into the links to curriculum, assessment and the learning theories and approaches appropriate for children at this stage of schooling, which are elaborated in subsequent chapters specific to the teaching of science and mathematics. To emphasise and encourage an active role on the part of the reader, at the end of Chapter 1 we have included a planning and reflecting teaching template, which contains a series of questions and considerations that every teacher must address. This template can be used to focus on decisions required for planning and successful teaching of each area, and draws attention to aspects related to curriculum, pedagogy and assessment. When using this template, you are encouraged to place yourself in the role of a practising teacher, preparing to teach and making important decisions. This template aligns with our philosophy as authors that it is important for individual teachers to plan and think about their own teaching approaches, and to find or adapt resources to their own contexts. This allows teachers to become reflective and reflexive practitioners, taking advantage of new ideas, resources and technologies. The template is also useful for tutorial activities with pre-service teachers, and would be helpful for in-service teachers seeking to refine or plan current or new units of work.

Chapter 2 provides an overview of ICT and its applications in teaching and learning in the early years of school. It covers a range of considerations that are important for teachers when using ICT with their young learners. The rapid development of ICT means that many of the resources available today might soon be redundant. For these reasons, we have avoided references to specific websites or resources where possible, and we encourage teachers to maintain currency in their personal ICT abilities and to model creativity, resilience and lifelong learning through their classroom ICT practices.

Chapters 3 to 8 deal with science in the early years of schooling, emphasising the development of science understandings, the nature of science, and science inquiry and literacy skills. Chapter 3 presents an overview of the strands of the science curriculum and draws attention to teachers' attitudes towards the teaching of science in the early years of schooling, while Chapters 4, 5, 6 and 7 address the four domains of the science curriculum: biological sciences, chemical sciences, earth and space science, and physical sciences. The chapters acknowledge that while specific understandings and concepts are prescribed by various curricula, the means of teaching these are not particularly prescriptive. At the beginning of each of these chapters and each targeted focus topic, the important science understandings are described. It is important that teachers consider how to make these understandings and ideas explicit to children through the learning episodes. While teachers should endeavour to align the requirements of the curriculum with the children's interests, it is also important to take the lead and facilitate new learning opportunities whenever possible. Chapter 8 presents additional science topics in which the integration of ICT is foregrounded in the teaching and learning process.

Chapters 9 to 13 deal with mathematics in the early years of schooling. Chapter 9 overviews key issues in the teaching and learning of mathematics, including play-based learning, questioning, and using routines and school contexts for building children's connected mathematics knowledge. It describes the importance of being mindful of the intuitive mathematical knowledge that children bring with them to school. Assessment of children's mathematics learning is also discussed. This chapter sets the scene for Chapters 10, 11 and 12, which present key concepts and ideas for promoting children's knowledge and understanding of number and algebra, statistics and probability, and geometry and measurement respectively. The strategies are designed to allow teachers to develop children's mathematical understanding, fluency, reasoning, and problem solving skills. In Chapter 13, we take a particular topic in the measurement strand—time—and elaborate the use of ICT to enhance students' learning of this topic.

Throughout each of the chapters, we have included sections labelled 'Teaching point'. These are designed to encourage further consideration of the teaching and learning processes involved in the episode, including links to other curriculum areas, types of questioning, assessment ideas, resources and practical considerations.

Teaching young children in the first three years of schooling

The first day of school

The first day of formal school is a highly emotional experience for children, and often for their parents. School is a place of high expectations, of meeting new friends, of playing in new environments, of using brand new pencils and other new equipment, and of becoming familiar with the routine of the day. There have often been weeks of preparation for school, resulting in a mounting sense of excitement and perhaps anxiety. On the first day of school, most young children arrive with expectations of learning—of becoming 'smart'. They have lofty career aspirations of becoming astronauts, doctors, firemen, palaeontologists, zookeepers, ballerinas or rock stars. They are brimming with a desire to learn. They look to the teacher to provide this.

When they begin formal schooling, many young children are ICT savvy. They know how to use a mobile phone and an iPad, how to scroll through screens to find their favourite game or app. They sometimes know how to count and share and measure. They have a sense of wonder and inquiry about the world around them. When young children come to school, they are poised to interact with technology to build and extend their mathematics and science knowledge.

The purpose of this chapter is to focus on some of the important aspects of teaching and learning that teachers need to consider in their daily work with young minds. This chapter overviews teaching strategies, questioning techniques, assessment strategies and curriculum integration, all of which are important regardless of the curriculum area in which a teacher works. These ideas are revisited and extended in more detail in each of the chapters on teaching science (Chapters 3 to 8) and teaching mathematics (Chapters 9 to 13).

Teaching strategies

There are many effective teaching strategies and learning environments that teachers can utilise when working with young learners. A central consideration that should be at the heart of teachers' decisions is how they can come to know, and capitalise and build upon, children's prior knowledge and their experiences beyond school. This constructivist approach not only allows children to make connections and construct their own knowledge; it also makes learning more authentic and relevant to the children.

According to Ausubel (1968), what a learner already knows has a significant impact on their future learning. The challenge for teachers is to elicit children's prior understandings. This can be done using many and varied strategies—for example, questioning, looking at children's drawings or making observations of children role-playing or using puppets to discuss their ideas (Campbell & Jobling 2012).

When planning to develop and build on children's understanding in any subject, the teacher should use as many varied and appropriate learning approaches and environments as possible. Play-based learning is a very important element of teaching and learning in the early years of school. It capitalises on children's natural skills and interests, as well as their instincts and questioning to learn. Play-based learning environments for mathematics are elaborated in Chapter 9, with detailed learning experiences to build and extend mathematical thinking given.

Using a play-based learning approach is not the only teaching strategy for the early years of school. The approaches adopted often depend on the nature of the learning and the concepts involved. For example, guided discovery or inquiry learning may be more appropriate than play-based activities for developing children's science understanding of certain topics. Further, school-based events provide rich contexts for learning. The teacher's role is to draw upon the context of the school to create rich learning experiences. For example, the school may be located by the sea, near a rainforest or in bushland; it may have a creek running beside it, or be located in the middle of a busy city centre. The school's surroundings provide immediate access to a plethora of resources and contexts for making learning more meaningful. Similarly, events such as sports day, the swimming carnival, the visiting circus and the dental van can become the focus for learning. Many schools have kitchen gardens that are part of a whole-school enterprise. The kitchen garden provides opportunities for learning both science and mathematics, which are only limited by a teacher's imagination and creativity. Specific teaching ideas and suggestions for developing young children's mathematics knowledge are presented in Chapter 9, with links to science in relation to hypothesising, experimenting, recording and analysing data, and drawing conclusions.

Not all valuable and important learning experiences are achievable through play-based discovery or inquiry activities. Sometimes, teacher-directed activities will be needed to scaffold the children's learning. While play-based, discovery, active or hands-on learning activities are integral to facilitating children's learning in the early grades, it is reasonable to expect that children will sometimes sit quietly and listen to you, the teacher and/or each other. It is important to remember that children's learning experiences need to be diverse, and for this reason it is not sufficient for a teacher to rely exclusively on direct instruction; however, we do our children no favours by not expecting that they will develop the skills of quiet observation and respectful listening.

Questioning

Much has been written about questioning, and we consider questioning to be one of the most important skills of an effective teacher. Questioning allows teachers to establish what children already know. It is an effective means of formatively assessing children's understanding on an ongoing basis. In addition, questioning can be used as an effective means of scaffolding children's learning, and it can prompt children's reasoning and extend their thinking. It takes time, effort and practice on the part of the teacher to develop good questioning skills and techniques. Questioning approaches can appear to be teacher-centred, however, the effective use of questioning, for example, hypothetical questioning or open-ended questions that prompt children to explore ideas or make tentative suggestions can create a child-centred learning situation (Department of Education and Training 2003).

Campbell and Jobling (2012) described the purposes of effective questioning in early years classrooms. These include:

- creating stimuli or impetus for exploration or investigation
- making predictions or hypothesising
- identifying existing knowledge and alternative conceptions
- promoting reasoning and argumentation
- encouraging discussion and problem-solving
- scaffolding thinking
- making observations.

They emphasise that the teacher need not always initiate the questions. Children can also generate many important and thought-provoking questions.

We encourage readers to explore online resources that are designed to support teachers in identifying and using effective questioning—see, for example, Jamie Mackenzie's questioning toolkit for teachers (Mackenzie 1997). Elaborations of questioning to extend children's thinking, reasoning and vocabulary specifically in relation to science and mathematics have been provided throughout the chapters, with examples given of teacher actions and learner experiences.

Assessment

Assessing learning in the first three years of schooling can be a complex task. It is, of course, important to determine what the child has learned through the experiences that have been facilitated. The type of evidence the teacher collects to determine a child's learning of a particular topic varies greatly, depending on the age of the child, their ability level, the topic, the concept or skill, the type of learning strategy engaged and the requirements of the education system. This means that one single assessment of a child's learning does not provide sufficient evidence upon which to draw conclusions about the child's learning. Teachers must collect data on children's learning from a variety of sources and using a variety of tools. Good assessment techniques also inform further teaching. Some possible assessment methods include the following.

Annotations

Teacher annotations in a journal of children's actions, behaviours and responses during activities can be a powerful means of informal, ongoing assessment, and can be applied to many of the activities described in all chapters of this book. Annotations cannot be completed for all children all the time, but a regular recording of these attributes will develop a clear picture over time. Try to record what the child can do and not what they cannot do. It is also necessary to give a clear context for the annotations so that in future the full meaning can be retained. Annotations can be made while children are participating in activities or responding to questions in group discussions (particularly open-ended questions).

Checklists
Similar to annotations, checklists can be a quicker method of recording a child's learning, but considerable thought is needed to predetermine the learning attributes on the list. In mathematics, for example, checklists can be constructed to monitor children's problem-solving and hence metacognitive skills. The four general stages of problem-solving—read and understand; make a plan; carry out the plan; and check reasonableness—with ratings of with help/without help can provide a teacher with a quick assessment as children undertake problem-solving tasks and inform planning for teaching. Similarly in science, checklists can be used to monitor children's acquisition of inquiry or questioning skills. Checklists are useful tools for tracking the development of children's ICT skills. In all subjects, checklists can be valuable for assessing children's social skills for group work, with such criteria as listens attentively, interrupts politely, takes turns, and values others suggestions providing key data for monitoring children's learning processes.

Written responses
For children who have advanced to be independent writers, much of their written work can be used for assessment. Written work can be viewed to determine a child's observations, predictions, descriptions, knowledge of important facts or language, and their conclusions or opinions. For children who are not yet writing, the teacher or class helper can transcribe their ideas as the children explain their thinking. Children should always be encouraged to reflect upon their learning experiences. Providing children with time to explain and describe their thinking processes sends important messages to students about the nature of the subject and what the teacher values about the subject.

Specific assessment tasks
The teacher may choose (where they deem it appropriate or necessary) to ask children to complete a prepared task sheet that requires them to demonstrate understanding of an aspect of their learning. From an early age, children learn to associate tests with feelings of self-worth. There are ways in which task sheets can effectively be disguised as fun learning tasks yet still provide specific assessment

TEACHING EARLY YEARS MATHEMATICS, SCIENCE AND ICT

data. Consider including 'fill the gap' sentences, puzzles, fun quizzes and coding tasks, as well as images of interesting characters and icons on task sheets.

Non-written representations

Children may create non-written representations such as role-plays, diagrams, illustrations, models and collections that reflect their understanding of both science and mathematics topics. Such activities can provide a dimension of fun and sharing for both assessment and learning. Non-written representations provide a range of opportunities for ICT assessment.

Student interviews

Student interviews can be very revealing. They can be as brief as a single question or more complex and probing. They occur while children are engaged in a learning activity, either individually or in a group. The teacher needs a clear idea of the focus of the interview, but also has to be prepared to diverge as the child completes explanations, descriptions, predictions, conclusions and opinions, or draws on their own background knowledge. Interviews can be recorded through brief notes on a prepared interview sheet or using software such as Soundnote.

Portfolios

A great deal of children's work can be gathered and filed in a portfolio as evidence of learning. Children like to have some control over their portfolio, so it may sometimes be appropriate to negotiate with a child as to what is kept. This is good experience for children's self-assessment and reflection. Sometimes, when one piece of work supersedes another, the child may wish the initial work to be removed, though this circumstance would also be excellent evidence of the child's progress. Dating the work is important to show how a child is progressing over a period of time.

Digital portfolios

A digital portfolio can be used in a similar way to a physical one. Photographing children's work is a good way of easily capturing a great deal of evidence of learning, and digital photos are easy to store and share. Children's own photographic collections can also be saved in this way. Paper-based work samples can also be scanned and saved in an electronic format to add further evidence to the digital portfolio.

Self-assessment

Children can self-assess in a number of ways—for example, through interviews or prepared pictogram criteria sheets needing a tick in the appropriate box. In the early years, smiley face icons appeal to students and can provide a window into how they feel about their own progress in relation to learning particular topics.

Planning and reflection teaching template

We have created a template intended for use in conjunction with each chapter or unit of work described in this text. The purpose of the template is to provoke you to reflect upon and make decisions about important elements of effective teaching. Each of the elements presented within this template highlights important considerations for teaching children in their first three years of schooling. Thus the template allows you to individualise the ideas for specific year levels, cohorts of children with particular needs and diversities, and particular school contexts. The template is shown in Table 1.1. During or after your reading of each chapter in this book, note your responses to each point on the template, to provide a comprehensive summary of the intent and key messages of each chapter.

Table 1.1 Reflection template for use with Chapters 4 to 8 and Chapters 10 to 13

For each chapter, respond to following points.	
Curriculum	• Examine your curriculum documents and identify the specific links to content and grade. • Examine other learning area curricula to identify cross-curricular learning possibilities (e.g. within a science chapter, what mathematics content might be included? What ICT or literacy could be included?)
Assessment	• Identify assessment possibilities and means of gathering, recording and/or reporting on evidence. Refer to the assessment section in Chapter 1 for descriptions of different assessment ideas.
Pedagogy	• Identify the teaching strategies outlined in the chapter and suggest alternative approaches that might be used in each context. (For example, rather than using discussion in a particular activity or content area, what else might you use?) • Think about some of the possible student diversities you may have in a cohort of children. Consider how you might adjust or adapt the approaches or learning episodes suggested to cater for such children.

For each chapter, respond to following points.		
Questioning	•	Identify the different types of questioning used. Consider whether you could or would use additional or other forms of questioning. Refer to the section in Chapter 1 for more information about different question types.
ICT	•	Find current ICT resources that would be beneficial to include in the teaching and learning in the science and mathematics chapters. Find new or alternative ICT resources for the activities presented in the ICT chapters.
Resources	•	What additional resources could you use effectively in the teaching of this unit (e.g. graphic organisers, books, human resources, physical or digital resources, manipulatives)?
Extension Ideas	•	How could the key concepts be extended or expanded to reinforce or deepen the children's learning? Extension means providing a wider range of learning opportunities (perhaps including more challenging ideas) about the same concept; it doesn't mean borrowing the concepts from the next year level in the syllabus.
Teachers' content knowledge and skills	•	If you feel that you need to expand or develop your own knowledge of a particular content area, or perhaps a particular approach or ICT, how might you go about doing this?

2

Information and communication technology in the first three years of schooling

Overview

Information and communication technology (ICT) is ubiquitous in our society. The majority of children entering formal schooling have interacted with ICT in many and varied ways. For teachers of children in the first three years of schooling, this presents a challenge but also a wonderful opportunity to ensure that ICT is an integral part of the teaching and learning process across all learning areas.

Different educational authorities may place varied emphases on ICT in early years classrooms. For instance, some see it as a discrete subject area while others combine it with a design focus. Still others require children to attain a set of capabilities that allow them to effectively interact with ICT. Whatever the systemic priorities, it is widely accepted that children learn to use ICT effectively when it is an integral part of their wider classroom learning. This makes the use of ICT authentic, and its valuable contribution to the teaching and learning of all subject areas in the classroom can be harnessed. When using ICT with children in the early years of schooling, there are a number of aspects that must be addressed. The ICT may be used to aid teaching and learning by accessing existing information (investigating), by making new products (creating) and by sharing information (communicating). Beyond this, children must also develop awareness of the need to manage ICT effectively, and use it in a safe and ethical way (Australian Curriculum, Assessment and Reporting Authority [ACARA] 2013). This chapter overviews a number of important considerations for the use of ICT in the first three years of schooling.

What is ICT?

In this book, the acronym ICT refers to the term 'information and communication technology'—both singular and plural. Where necessary, the acronym ICTs is used as the plural form. Alternative terminology with similar meaning may be encountered in educational literature—for instance 'digital technologies', 'new technologies' and 'educational technologies'. The term 'ICT' includes a set of tools and systems that allow our society to access, generate and share information. These tools and systems include hardware such as computers and tablets, software such as learning games and applications (apps) and systems and networks, including the internet. As far as early years classrooms are concerned, ICT is a term that refers to any digital tool that supports the teaching and learning process by allowing the teacher and children to investigate, create, share and manage information.

The big picture

ICT has become a vital aspect of modern economies. Most countries now place great emphasis on 'knowledge economies'. A literate, numerate and digitally literate citizenry is key to developing an economy that can keep pace with a rapidly changing world. As with so many aspects of learning, the experiences that children in the early years of schooling have with ICT are critical in establishing future success for themselves and their society.

Young users of ICT

Most children's early experiences of using ICT have been through the notion of play. Young children enjoy their interactions with ICT as entertainment—for example, watching a video on an iPad or playing a game on the computer. As with the broader philosophy of learning in the first years of schooling, play has a vital role.

Children willingly engage in play activities, and through their explorations they become familiar with using ICT, developing digital technology skills such as using a mouse, menus and toolbars, and becoming familiar with software (Zevenbergen & Logan 2008). Knowing this, teachers can harness the children's natural desire to play to broaden the learning base with ICT, both generally and with specific programs (Sheridan & Pramling Samuelsson 2003).

With young learners, it is also beneficial whenever possible to relate what they are doing in the virtual world to the real world. For instance, if children are making 3D models in a software program, it is advantageous to also work with 'real' 3D modelling—for example, by using blocks or play dough (Lee & O'Rourke 2006).

Learning benefits from ICT

Many ICT resources have specific benefits for learning; however, a number of broader learning benefits are afforded through thoughtful classroom use of ICT. Learning is seen as socially constructed—that is, we learn a great deal from our interactions with others. If children are given the opportunity to work together using ICT, then this socially constructed learning can be enhanced through social interactions, which can subsequently benefit language development. Children also have the opportunity to teach each other and share their knowledge, which can be a very powerful learning experience. There are various ways to promote group and collaborative work with young children while using ICT, through such activities as sharing a computer or mobile device, or collaborative problem-solving using the interactive whiteboard (IWB).

Figure 2.1 (a) Computer sharing; (b) collaborating with the IWB

Teacher challenges

Teachers face numerous challenges in effectively integrating ICT into early years classrooms. As with all challenges, attitude can be a major indicator of success. There are ICT-related issues that must be addressed on numerous levels:

- the teacher's personal skills and abilities with ICT
- the availability of ICT in the classroom
- the ICT support provided, such as maintenance and training
- the cohort of children and their access and prior experiences with ICT and
- wider influences, such as education authority policies and government funding.

Some of these issues are beyond the control of the teacher, but they still need to be understood.

Teachers' personal competence with ICT is an advantage but not necessarily pivotal to success: a great player of a sport does not always make a great coach. With reasonably good personal ICT skills, a positive attitude, and thoughtful and creative lesson planning, a teacher can deliver wonderfully rich teaching and learning experiences to their classes. Attitudes of resilience and patience are required when working with ICT, as there will often be glitches with hardware, software or systems that may interrupt the best of plans. Modelling these positive characteristics to the children is all part of their learning with ICT. It is almost impossible to be an expert in all aspects of ICT, not least because of the rapidity with which new ICT develops. However, this can be viewed as an opportunity rather than a barrier: learning about ICT alongside the children is a great opportunity to model the attributes of a lifelong learner.

Home and school

It is important for teachers to determine the children's prior and current experiences with ICT. It is good to know what access children have to ICT in the home and community, how they use it and the skills they may have—for instance, can they use the internet? Can they use a digital camera? Are they aware of safety protocols?

The concept of 'digital divide' is interesting to consider here. The term initially referred to the divide that existed between the digital 'haves' and 'have nots' (an economic differentiation), but today it also refers to the difference between the ICT that children use at school and that used out of school (Buckingham 2005). In an increasing number of cases, children have access to far more sophisticated

ICT away from school, which can lead to disinterest in, or disengagement from, the school-based ICT. This returns the onus to the teacher. While sometimes not able to control the type of ICT available in the school or classroom, the teacher can control how it is used to make it an engaging contributor to children's learning.

By contrast, there are some children whose only access to ICT is at school. This situation creates an imperative for the teacher to ensure that these children are given every opportunity to use and learn from ICT.

ICT infrastructure

The way in which ICT is made available in schools may sometimes be out of the teacher's control. The quantity, quality and classroom availability of ICT vary from school to school. As a staff member, you can make suggestions about improvements, but the usual scenario is that the teacher makes the best use of what is available while always looking for opportunities to increase access and support for their young learners. Much less expensive devices are now making it increasingly possible for classes to be autonomous with their ICT, though in many schools sharing resources is still a way of life. Sharing computers, either through sets of devices on trolleys, or library and laboratory classrooms, controls to some extent the pedagogy the teacher employs and the ways in which children engage with the ICT. Some examples include:

- *Mini labs and banks of computers.* These are usually four to six computers for children to use. This might be in an adjoining room that is shared with another class or it might be a bank of computers along a wall in the classroom. Small groups of children can rotate through these computers.
- *School computer laboratories.* The computers are generally identical, with the same setup allowing all children access to the same computer programs and internet sites. As all children are generally completing the same activities, it is easy for the teacher to provide the necessary scaffolding when teaching.
- *Mobile ICT.* A 'computers on wheels' (COWs) setup allows laptops or other devices to be moved easily from class to class. These devices are also generally identical and configured in the same way so that all computers in the 'class set' are identical.

Whichever ICT infrastructure is available, it is important to ensure that teachers and children are aware of protocols for use so that they and subsequent users of the ICT are not disadvantaged.

14 TEACHING EARLY YEARS MATHEMATICS, SCIENCE AND ICT

Figure 2.2 A child using a laptop computer

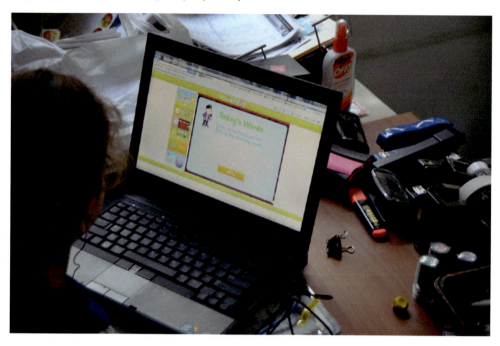

Figure 2.3 A class computer laboratory.

Pedagogical adaptations and innovations

When a teacher has assessed their own ICT abilities, the ICT abilities of their young class and the available ICT, the planning for teaching and learning can begin. With ICT in mind, the critical question the teacher must address is 'Will integrating particular ICT enhance the teaching and learning experience?' The answer to this is not always clear-cut, but ICT should at least be considered.

When choosing to use ICT as part of children's learning the teacher must consider whether there is a need for a pedagogical change that would enhance the experience. For instance, research has shown that some teachers when using an IWB simply project notes and exercises on to the IWB that they previously would have written on a chalkboard: in essence, nothing changed. Good teaching is not simply a matter of 'adding technology to the existing teaching and content domain' (Koehler & Mishra 2005, p. 134). The IWB has the potential to deliver many enhanced learning experiences if the teacher considers how to harness them through pedagogical adaptation. Teachers must be prepared to modify their teaching practices to accommodate the introduction of new ICT (Hennessy et al. 2005; Hobbs 2006).

Teachers in the early years of schooling need knowledge of the content they are to teach and an understanding of pedagogies that work best with young children. They also must know how to use ICT to enhance and interweave both of these areas with a positive attitude for experimentation and risk-taking (Kimber & Wyatt-Smith 2006). Content knowledge refers to subject-matter knowledge, while pedagogical knowledge encompasses 'deep knowledge about the processes and practices or methods of teaching and learning' (Mishra & Koehler 2006, p. 1026). When a teacher understands how to effectively incorporate ICT with these two factors the result is known as technological pedagogical and content knowledge (TPACK) (Mishra & Koehler 2006).

Sometimes ICT can deliver completely new means of learning to the classroom, and the teacher may need to become very innovative with their pedagogies. An example of this was the introduction of movie-making software as standard on new computers; this was a powerful tool that had never been available in regular classrooms before but had enormous potential to enhance teaching and learning.

An interesting aspect of learning with some games, apps or software is that the child does not have to follow a linear thought process. With most reading books, for example, the plot is linear: the child starts at the beginning and works through to the end. This helps to develop logical and sequential thinking; however, many ICT resources have been designed to be non-linear, allowing the child's thinking to move in different directions (associative ways) and thus enabling the development of creative thinking patterns (Sheridan & Pramling Samuelsson 2003). Being aware of these factors allows the teacher to make pedagogically sound choices for teaching and learning (Hilton 2007; Hilton & Hilton 2013).

Integration across the curriculum

It is important for young children to learn *about* ICT—for instance, how to complete simple and safe internet searches, how to file and organise their work and how to physically use equipment. Children need these basic skills to move effectively to learning *with* ICT. The true power of ICT in the early years classrooms (or any classroom) is that there are now available almost limitless resources with which children can investigate topics across the curriculum, exciting ways of creating new products in all learning areas and dynamic means of sharing their learning with an audience.

When integrating ICT across the curriculum, the teacher needs to have a clear understanding of the purpose of the ICT's inclusion. A science topic about various environments of the world may be introduced through an age-appropriate video allowing children to see, hear and discuss. Further learning may occur with simple internet searches of particular countries, or by using apps on iPads with pictures and information. Children may make collections of digital images and information to create a file of what they have discovered. They may then use a communication format, such as PowerPoint, or image-presentation software to share their learning with others. Different ICT require particular thought by the teacher as to which would best suit the intended lesson objectives, what would be engaging and exciting, and what would add value to the learning experience.

When planning ways to effectively integrate ICT into class lessons, the teacher needs to consider a number of factors. A checklist of these factors could include:

Pre-lesson:

- Incorporate ICT integration into lesson planning.
- Plan a gradual introduction with new or unfamiliar ICT.
- Use support networks of fellow teachers or the library, as well as online teacher networks (many educational authorities facilitate these) for guidance.
- Determine the role of the ICT: is it for investigating, creating or communicating?

- Identify skills needing to be taught before effective use is possible.
- Decide how children use ICT—individually or in groups.

During the lesson:
- Be flexible if the ICT doesn't function as you wished; have a back-up plan.
- Guide children to help them develop new learning experiences and understandings of the world.

After the lesson:
- Reflect on the benefits of the ICT inclusion.
- Consider changes, developments or incremental steps for future use.

Figure 2.4 Integration of ICT into the early years classroom (robotics)

Teacher-generated ICT resources

ICT does not have to be pre-packaged for use in early years classrooms. Teachers can use ICT to create resources specifically tailored to learning goals and the needs of their classes or individuals. Creating IWB presentations with images, sound bites and hyperlinks specifically aligned with learning activities can greatly enhance the experience by reiterating ideas and concepts, or leading children to new ideas and knowledge.

Teachers who create their own learning activities for their class afford greater flexibility and more targeted experiences for the learner. Teachers have always prepared lessons and learning experiences for their classes; being able to harness the power of ICT for this purpose is a wonderful addition to a teacher's skills. Creating activities with the IWB, making podcasts with iPhoto and GarageBand, making movies with iMovie and making learning sequences with a home page and links to resources and activities (Campbell & Scotellaro 2009) are powerful tools in the hands of a creative and skilful teacher.

Teachers can also use ICT effectively for the administration of their classes. For example, at a parent–teacher event, a Year 1 teacher places images of each child on a display board. Each image has a QR code attached; the parents use their mobile phones with the QR code to access their child's digital portfolio of classroom activities and work samples.

Evaluating ICT for use with children in the first years of school

To ensure the best ICT is used in the best possible way for maximum teaching and learning benefit, it is important to have criteria for selection. This applies particularly when choosing software, websites and apps. Ensure that the resources with which students work are age- and culturally appropriate, engaging, provide clear instructions and allow the user to pause, save and continue. These choices can be made by the teacher, although sometimes where appropriate the teacher can engage the children in the decision-making process to help them become safer and more aware users of ICT. An example given by Lee and O'Rourke (2006) focuses on an issue where accents used in particular software originated from elsewhere in the world. The teachers used this as an opportunity to help children to be critically literate about the possible strengths and weaknesses, or the appropriateness, of the software in their own context.

When choosing hardware for children in the early years, ensure that it is appropriate for their level of manual dexterity, hand–eye coordination, and fine and gross motor skills. Some of the more recent innovations with tablet devices are excellent for young learners in this regard.

Below are some criteria to help determine whether an ICT is appropriate for the classroom.

Content
- Is the content accurate and educationally appropriate for the children?
- Will the content meet the learning intentions or learning outcomes of the lesson?

ICT IN THE FIRST THREE YEARS OF SCHOOLING   19

Figure 2.5   A child using a tablet device

Useability
- Are the instructions easy to understand and age appropriate?
- Can the children start/stop and exit at any time?
- Can the children or the teacher set the instructional level?

Quality
- Are the graphics, animations, audio and video of a high standard and appropriate for the lesson?
- Is the feedback to the children appropriate and positive?

Purpose
- Will the purpose of the software, website or app meet the outcomes of the lesson?

Other
- Does the education authority allow access to the website, software or app?
- Is a site licence needed?

Matching ICT resources to learning objectives

The vast variety of ICT learning resources available today, such as software, websites and apps, allows the teacher to be very specific about the role these resources play in children's learning. Some examples follow.

- *Drill and practice resources* provide exercises for children in most curriculum areas, but particularly in mathematics, spelling and grammar. These resources usually allow children to improve speed and/or accuracy. They generally are designed to work within children's existing knowledge, but may have competency levels to cater for diverse learners. To maintain children's interest, these resources usually have engaging formats with positive feedback for success.
- *ICT teaching resources* are designed to lead children through a topic that is new to them. These resources should allow the child to progress by themselves and at their own pace. Because children in the early years of schooling initially often have limited reading ability, these ICT teaching resources must be designed using multiple representations rather than just text. Research provides strong evidence that the use of multiple representations in a variety of modes is a powerful support for conceptual development. It also assists children to become familiar with multiple literacies—literacies beyond those associated with text.
- *Instructional games* can be similar to ICT drill and practice teaching resources, but they include an element of competition that many children find very engaging. The competition can be a child vying for a personal best or against another class member. In some online games, the child may compete with children in other locations around the world. Some of these instructional games can also be programmed by the teacher to ensure that the focus is on relevant and current learning topics.
- *Problem-solving ICT resources* are excellent for engaging students in higher order thinking. Rather than requiring the child to simply remember or reproduce facts and information, these resources require children to apply their knowledge in new contexts that require them to make connections or develop strategies.

Assessment of children's use of ICT

Children will use ICT with varying levels of proficiency, with the curriculum giving an idea of the expected benchmarks. As the use of ICT in early years of schooling involves children's ability to find new knowledge, make products that demonstrate their knowledge, and then share and manage the products, the assessment of their abilities should reflect these emphases.

Methods of assessment (as articulated in Chapter 1) may include maintaining a digital portfolio of products, anecdotal records or a checklist of required ICT skills. (The checklist can be arranged in levels—for example, 'Can work independently', 'Can work with peer assistance' or 'Can work with teacher assistance'). For some aspects of ICT skills development, such as safety, ethical protocols and operating skills, a checklist is often the simplest and most appropriate form of assessment.

Teacher learning with ICT

The process of incorporating ICT effectively into an early years classroom can be a developmental one for the teacher as well as the student. The impact of new and emerging ICT on the teaching and learning process can be complex (Metiri Group 2006). Often teachers will begin using ICT in a modest way, keeping things simple, but as their confidence and experience grow, more complex use of ICT can be developed. In the initial stages, teachers sometimes like to simply 'try' an ICT without making many pedagogical changes. Once the 'mechanics' of the ICT are familiar, confidence grows to support more innovative uses. Again, this requires a positive attitude to attempt new things and not be disheartened if at first things don't work as planned.

Unique affordances of ICT

ICT has brought new learning opportunities to classrooms. Some examples that have changed the teaching and learning experience include simulations and animations, robotics and digital cameras. Beyond the particular affordances of specific devices, ICT has been shown (when used wisely) to benefit children's learning through its ability to differentiate, catering for multiple learning styles and learning rates.

Simulations and animations

Simulations and animations provide great opportunities for children to engage with all kinds of phenomena, and they are excellent for allowing visualisation of processes. In science, for example, animations and simulations are useful alternatives if actual scientific equipment is too costly, not available or difficult for children to manipulate. Sometimes they are preferable because they simplify a phenomenon, making it easier for children to understand, visualise or discuss. Simulations and animations can be especially useful to support children's visualisation of processes that are not easily observed because of the speed with which they occur. In such cases, children can often be exposed to both real and simulated worlds. For example, growing plants is a very slow process, which children enjoy, but because of its slowness, changes can be difficult for children to observe directly. Coupling this experience with digital simulations of plant growth can enhance children's understanding. This same approach can be used for processes that occur too quickly to be observed easily. For example, the actions of a bee landing on flowers and collecting pollen can be difficult to see, but a simulation or animation can provide another opportunity for children to watch how the bee uses different parts of its body to go about this task. These are examples of integrating ICT into the natural learning environment. Research has shown that using pedagogically appropriate ICT in this way is a powerful means of supporting and enhancing learning experiences for children (Gialamas & Nikolopoulou 2010).

Using simulations and animations can promote positive attitudes. They also help to develop children's ability to visualise and to understand concepts more deeply. While simulations and animations can provide valuable learning experiences, there are some things about which teachers need to be aware when using them. Simulations have advantages over animations because they allow children to change variables in different ways and observe the outcomes of their choices. The decision to use animations and simulations also requires other considerations—for example, are there differences between the model and reality? Does something happen differently in the model than it would in reality? If the answer is yes to such questions, the teacher may need to point these things out to the children to avoid the possibility of them forming misconceptions.

Robotics

Robotics in schools has been widely acknowledged as enhancing student learning outcomes—especially motivation, engagement and problem-solving skills. Particularly suited to the younger years are Bee-bots. These are robots that are programmable, which is a unique affordance bringing new skills and problem-solving to the learning experience. For example, when placed on the floor after programming, Bee-bots can be used to promote the learning and ordering of numbers as they move along floor mats. As robots continue to develop, children will have opportunities to experience a variety of learning experiences with more robots that have increased functionality.

Figure 2.6 Children testing robots

Robotics has been found to enhance young children's learning in mathematics in the areas of direction, angles, estimation, shape, and spatial awareness. Using robotics with children also facilitates group and collaborative work. Digital storytelling can be incorporated if the robots are integrated into the curriculum and used to tell a story. These stories can then be video-recorded using class cameras or mobile devices such as iPads. These productions can be shared within the class and with other classes, and can become part of a digital portfolio for sharing with parents or the wider community.

Learner response systems in the classroom

Learner response systems, are devices such as clickers or online programs or apps that allow each child to simultaneously answer a question asked by the teacher. The associated software allows the class teacher (and the children) to see the results for each question asked. This shows the teacher whether the children understand the concepts being taught or if further work needs to be completed on the topic. Discussion can be promoted through their use, and there are various techniques that can provide feedback to the teacher. These include asking multiple-choice questions, true/false, short-answer or single-word open-ended questions. Some systems also have sort and ordering activities that can be created for the children using the software provided.

Learner response systems are becoming more popular in schools, particularly with teachers of young children. They can be helpful for teachers in catering for individual differences in the classroom, thereby ensuring the inclusion of all children.

The future

Teachers' positive and resilient attitudes towards the use of ICT in the early years of schooling will also be required for the challenges of future ICT development. When considering the advancements in ICT over the last ten years, and the impact ICT has had on classroom practice, one can hardly imagine what future classroom ICT will entail. For example, while the internet has revolutionised the connectedness of people, the next phase is the connectedness of things (objects communicating with each other), which will again revolutionise the way the world functions, with resulting ramifications for teaching and learning. Professional learning opportunities for teachers will usually be available, but this is never enough to maintain currency of practice—especially with ICT. It will be necessary, as it has always been with teaching, to take personal responsibility for ongoing/lifelong learning to ensure that the children we teach obtain maximum learning benefits from our expertise.

Science in the first three years of schooling

Overview

Children have a natural curiosity about the world around them. According to French (2004), young children are biologically prepared and motivated to engage with and learn about the everyday world, especially through social interactions and experiences. The challenge for teachers of children in the first three years of schooling is to tap into and preserve their students' innate curiosity and desire to learn science (Raffini 1993).

The following chapters about teaching and learning science are not meant to be comprehensive or prescriptive. They are designed to give an insight into some ways of thinking as a teacher of science for young school children. The skill, joy and creativity of teaching science comes with adapting ideas and opportunities to suit a particular context, interest or cohort of students. These elements constantly change, so it isn't always possible to articulate 'what works' in early school years science classes. It is only possible to give examples of 'what can work' in an ever-changing mix of interests, abilities and knowledges of both teacher and student. While giving some guidance to the teaching of science topics, these chapters are better viewed as a springboard for your own ideas. Teaching science using your own great ideas and being responsive to your students' knowledge and interests will bring great pleasure to the teaching and learning process.

Four content areas of science understanding are addressed here:

- biological science
- chemical science
- earth and space science
- physical science.

Each of these areas is described in one of the following four chapters; however, it is important to consider that it is often not possible to keep these four content areas discrete—in fact, some overlapping or intertwining of the four areas more closely reflects the situation in the real world. Within each of the four areas, we have presented two topics or units of work to illustrate teaching approaches that may be used in science teaching in the early years. The teaching and learning episodes articulated within the units do not specify a year level, but can be adjusted to suit the specific cohort of children across the first three years of school.

Just as it is difficult to focus on discrete subject areas within science, so too is it often very difficult to isolate science learning from other key learning areas in the early years of schooling. The notion of 'taking a science lesson' is not the norm. Usually, the activities involved in developing understanding of the nature of science, science concepts and science inquiry skills are inextricably linked and beneficial to developing numeracy, literacy, technology and design, or interpersonal skills and behaviours. In many cases, science activities can provide authentic reasons and opportunities for developing skills in some of these areas.

What is science?

The word 'science' can relate to the body of knowledge known as 'science' and the set of skills known as 'science' (Zimmerman 2000)—for example, knowing about coral reproduction and performing the skills of observing, collecting data, representing and interpreting the information about coral can both be referred to as 'science'. Put simply, the word 'science' can refer to the 'knowing' and the 'doing', or the 'conceptual' and the 'procedural'. Children in the first years of schooling can benefit from understanding particular science concepts as well as developing skills and language from completing science procedures. Science is emergent: it develops through doing (Siry et al. 2012).

Where appropriate, the learning sequences in Chapters 4 to 8 include reference to:

- the specific science understandings, which can be thought of as the focus concepts or content
- the nature of science, where the benefit of science to humankind is emphasised and the ways in which scientists' work can be illustrated
- the science inquiry skills required for the successful undertaking of scientific thinking and doing, and
- scientific literacy skills.

Scientists use scientific ways of thinking and doing to understand things ranging from atoms, genes and pathogens to black holes and earthquakes. New scientific areas are developing as scientific discoveries advance our knowledge—for example, genomics and nanotechnology. This is at the heart of the nature of science, which is something very important for children to appreciate as they learn science through their years at school. First, scientific knowledge is tentative and changing—it is not just a fixed bank of knowledge; second, scientific knowledge and techniques develop because of research and creativity (scientists asking questions and looking for evidence and creative ways to answer their questions); and finally, scientists' work impacts on the world and is influenced by society and culture, and expectations such as ethics.

Scientific literacy has been defined and redefined over recent decades. The OECD includes in its definition of scientific literacy the use of scientific knowledge to explain phenomena, identify scientific issues, understand how science influences our world and engage with science and scientific issues as a reflective citizen (Bybee & McCrae 2011). While these attributes may seem beyond the goals of teachers in the early years of school, teachers in these years can begin to build the foundations on which these attributes can develop. It is also widely acknowledged that science students need generic literacy skills such as interpreting images and text, contributing to group discussion, creating texts (such as reports and PowerPoints), and noticing patterns in evidence. According to Prain and Waldrip (2010), it is the development of these literacy skills in science contexts that are crucial contributors to students' scientific literacies. They add that scientific literacies include scientific language practices, which include using visual, verbal, mathematical and other representations.

Teachers' attitudes to science

In the following chapters, it is intended that the teaching and learning episodes will be viewed as templates for teachers' thinking about the world with young children's science learning in mind. A teacher who develops personal habits of mind to constantly wonder at the world will be better equipped to share their joy of discovery and learning with their students. Wondrous and beautiful teaching and learning opportunities often await in seemingly mundane aspects of our daily lives.

Sadly, though, research has shown that in the first years of school, some teachers avoid teaching science (Watters & Ginns 2000). This can be attributed to a number of possible causes:

- The teacher may need a clearer understanding of what is entailed in science learning in these years.
- They may require further understanding of where and how science exists in children's everyday lives.
- They may need to better recognise and develop children's natural engagement in science (Fleer 2009).

The following chapters will assist in addressing these issues.

Effective teachers of science in the early years of schooling require diverse skills. They must understand the nature of science, age-appropriate science content, how young students learn science and the pedagogies required to engage them. Don't be daunted by this: as a teacher, you will spend your lifetime teaching, learning and reflecting on ways and means of refining these skills. This is not a bad thing—it is what excites teachers: finding creative ways to engage learners. You do not need to be a scientist or have an extensive scientific background or training; rather, you need to be able to ask questions and make observations, and think about and look for patterns in the world around you.

Should we teach science in the early years of schooling?

The argument against

Debate exists as to whether students in the early years of schooling should be taught science, with some arguing that these students are not developmentally ready for the rigours of scientific thinking. For instance, while being able to experience concepts such as force, velocity and acceleration, are children in the early years of school capable of understanding these concepts—especially as many of these concepts involve counter-intuitive thinking (Wolpert 1992)?

Additionally, concern has been expressed that young students could easily develop scientific misconceptions that may be very difficult to unlearn in later years (Gardner 1999). While these concerns exist or have existed, the outlook is actually far more positive and exciting.

The argument for

Today it is felt that young learners can benefit from learning science. They are capable of creative and divergent thinking, both of which can be stimulated by science learning. Two traditional justifications have driven the argument for teaching science in the early years of schooling: that science engages children in the real world, and that it helps develop scientific ways of thinking (Eshach & Fried 2005). While these notions seem reasonable, the teaching and learning of science in the early years of schooling entails much more, as Eshach and Fried (2005, pp. 319–30) summarised:

- Children naturally enjoy observing and thinking about nature. Even when playing, they engage in aspects of science such as observing, attending to or collecting.
- Exposing children to science develops positive attitudes that are important for future engagement in science.
- Early exposure to scientific phenomena leads to better understanding of the scientific concepts studied later in a more formal way.
- The careful introduction of scientifically informed language at an early age influences the development of scientific concepts by helping children to understand and communicate what they are observing, and to transfer knowledge to new contexts or phenomena.
- Children can understand scientific concepts and reason scientifically. They are also able to connect observations and evidence to theory.
- Science is an efficient means for developing scientific thinking. As science concepts and procedures are linked by reasoning and thinking, both analytically and critically, they can develop together with the child.

Methods of engaging children in science

As children engage in the world around them, they will intentionally or unintentionally participate in learning science concepts and procedures. A teacher of science in the first three years of schooling has numerous teaching approaches from which to choose to guide or facilitate this learning. An emphasis on a particular teaching approach may be recommended or mandated by the curriculum, may be more suited to a particular topic, age level and cohort, or may be part of a teacher's philosophy and practice. Teaching approaches include, but are not limited to, play and guided play, direct teaching and guidance, questioning and demonstrating. In the following chapters, the teaching approaches for various teaching and learning episodes are articulated to give a broad understanding of possible means of engaging science learning. Needless to say, whichever method a teacher uses to engage young children in science, it must be done with care.

Resources for science teaching

A greater range of resources is readily available on the internet and through school libraries, or from community facilities such as museums. Selecting an age-appropriate storybook aligned with the topic is a great way of introducing or concluding a teaching sequence or for generating discussion. Finding powerful up-to-date websites can provide excellent support to investigating many topics. The list of possibilities is endless, and it is important that the teacher consider the best resources to complement the science.

While these chapters maintain a focus on the real world through activities with which children can physically engage, the benefit of incorporating additional virtual resources can be profound. As well as being an integral part of scientific research, communicating and sharing, ICT can allow children to experience things previously unavailable in the learning process, such as the micro or macro worlds in simulations and animations.

Throughout the science episodes, we have provided a range of images that are intended to illustrate particular ideas or to guide the reader in the use of images to prompt children's ideas or discussion, to assist in the development of concepts, and to support children's predictions, wondering and hypothesising. The reader should also look at these images with a view to thinking about how they might collect images themselves that can become part of their own set of teaching resources. We encourage the reader to think about topics within and beyond science where the use of images can be a powerful contributor to children's learning experiences.

4
Biological science

Biological science focuses on understanding living things—their structure and function, how they interact with each other and their surroundings, and reproduction, biodiversity and evolution. Clearly, these areas are complex and in many cases involve abstract concepts. It is the job of a teacher of the early years of school to introduce children to these ideas and to select appropriate activities that will help them start to develop the vocabulary, understanding and questioning abilities that will allow them to build on their initial learning in this area of science as they progress through school. In this chapter, the focus is on nature and building on the children's current ideas and experiences to help them establish an understanding of the diversity of living things and how they respond or adapt to their environments to help them survive.

Integration of mathematics and ICT into biological science

In this chapter, the integration of mathematics and ICT includes, but is not limited to:

- *Number and Algebra:* basic number concepts and counting
- *Geometry and Measurement:* construction of 2D shapes, informal measurement of length, time intervals (minutes)
- *Statistics and Probability:* data collection, representation in tables and graphs, using data to inform decisions
- *ICT:* digital cameras to capture images; IWB for creating, discussing and displaying data; viewing of online materials; presentation software (e.g. PowerPoint) for

32   TEACHING EARLY YEARS MATHEMATICS, SCIENCE AND ICT

communicating; online searches for investigating and gathering information; other software and apps as appropriate.

BIOLOGICAL SCIENCE I ─────────────────

Animal homes

- **Science understanding:** Animals have differing needs for shelter, which may relate to shelter from physical or environmental elements, such as heat, wind, rain, and cold, or perhaps from predators or to protect their young.
- **Nature of science:** Exploring and observing our environment and looking for patterns; using science to help care for the environment.

OVERVIEW

In this unit, the idea of a 'home' is investigated as it pertains to animals. Through this unit, children will explore the idea of animal homes: their purposes, similarities and differences. Characteristics of homes and their locations can be related to their purposes. For example, a home built for protection from the weather (e.g. a bear's cave) may differ from one intended mainly for protection from predators (e.g. a bird's nest). Links can be made to the importance of protecting animals and their homes/habitats. The ideas can be used as the basis for future understandings about the distinction between consequences to an individual animal of the loss of its home and the impact on a species of the loss of habitat.

EPISODE I ···

What is a home?

Class discussion

SCIENCE INQUIRY SKILLS   *Respond to questions, discuss and share ideas*

Focus the unit of work by reading *The Three Little Pigs*. Direct an ensuing discussion about the story—for example, what materials did the pigs use to build their houses; why were some successful and some not; what materials would they (the children) use to build a home and why?

> **Teaching point:** This activity provides an opportunity to engage in basic number development and to develop children's literacy skills.

BIOLOGICAL SCIENCE 33

Broaden the discussion

SCIENCE INQUIRY SKILLS *Respond to questions and reason*
SCIENTIFIC LITERACY   *Scientific vocabulary development*

Gather children's ideas to create a word wall (perhaps with pictures) or posters displaying their ideas about questions such as: What is a home? What is a home used for? Why are homes important? This could be done using IWB presentation formats—for example, Wordle, PowerPoint.

Activity

SCIENCE INQUIRY SKILLS *Represent ideas and communicate*
SCIENTIFIC LITERACY   *Scientists use diagrams to represent and organise observations*

Children draw their own homes, then label and annotate (with or without assistance) the parts of their home and describe why they like their home, before sharing with other children. Children can share what they know about the homes of people who live in different parts of the world. Using the homes shown in Figure 4.1 (or similar collection) ask children to explain how they differ in some ways but not in others.

> **Teaching point:** In this activity, children have the opportunity to develop mathematical concepts related to differing shapes and sizes while drawing their homes.

> **Teaching point:** In this episode, the teacher uses discussion to introduce the topic and also determines what the children already know through questioning. By doing this, the teacher is better able to scaffold children's links from current knowledge to new learning. Questioning has also been used to encourage reasoning. Children represent their ideas through drawing and labelling. These drawings could be collected to assist with assessment.

EPISODE 2

Do animals have homes?

Class discussion

SCIENCE INQUIRY SKILLS *Make predictions, pose questions and respond*

With reference to *The Three Little Pigs*, do pigs really build their own homes? Do animals live in homes? What animals build homes? What animals don't build homes? Why do some animals build homes and not others? Develop a class list of animals and homes

Figure 4.1 Human homes may look different in different parts of the world, but they have some similarities of purpose

that children know. Determine what else children would like to know about animals and their homes.

> **Teaching point:** Here the questioning moves from closed (yes/no or factual answer) to open-ended types requiring children to think and respond in greater depth. The final question in this section can lead children's choice of investigation, which can promote powerful learning.

This activity could be done using a KWHL chart (K = What I know; W= What I would like to know; H = How I can find this out; L = What I've learned). An IWB could be used here. Look for sample templates online.

Viewing

SCIENCE INQUIRY SKILLS *Observe and compare*

Develop a set of image resources around 'Animal Homes' (with or without children's help) to use as discussion starters. Figure 4.2 shows some examples. Children can look for similarities and differences of home characteristics—for example, constructed homes such as nests or existing safe places such as caves, types of construction materials, and whether the home is for one creature or many. Where do some creatures build their homes—for example, in trees, underground, at the water's edge or on cliffs? Lead the discussion towards constructing a definition of a home. This may lead to some contentious issues, such as whether a shell or a carapace is a home.

> **Teaching point:** This kind of discussion and questioning can help develop children's reasoning from current knowledge. It allows teachers to help children avoid misconceptions prompted by stories or images in which snails 'carry their homes on their backs' by clarifying that a shell is not a home, but is in fact part of the animal.

Matching activity

SCIENCE INQUIRY SKILLS *Use senses and reason, classify*

Using words or images, have children match an animal to its home or home type. Discuss type, size, location and materials in matching the animal to the home. Perhaps the reasons why the animal has chosen the materials or the uses of the home could be discussed as an extension of the matching activity. This activity could be done well using the IWB touch and drag function.

Figure 4.2 Some constructed animal homes

Classification activity

SCIENCE INQUIRY SKILLS *Classify*

This activity can be done in many ways, and can be repeated on different days with different classifications. Using separate spaces in the classroom (string circles or hoops are good) and pictures of animals, children can name and classify animals and their home characteristics—for example, animals that use homes and those that don't; animals that construct homes and those that use existing safe places such as caves, tree holes or hollow logs.

BIOLOGICAL SCIENCE 37

> **Teaching point:** There may be some discussion about the definition of a home—for example, a koala lives in a tree but is the tree a home; whales live in the sea but can we call the sea a home? This may lead to discussion of home and habitat. The point does not have to be resolved, but simply discussed.

Field trip

SCIENCE INQUIRY SKILLS *Explore, observe, collect, record, and use digital technologies and share*

Explore the school grounds or a nearby park. Look for examples of animal homes. Emphasise and discuss with the children the need to 'look but don't touch' for the sake of the animal as well as personal safety. In these environments, close inspection can reveal numerous insect and bird homes. Also look for signs of creatures that perhaps don't use a home. Take one or more digital cameras to record findings. On return to class, create group or class slideshows showing the animals and their homes with pertinent labels or annotations. Share the slide shows.

> **Teaching point:** This is an example of guided discovery, where the teacher and children investigate together. Skamp (2008) notes that children have a strong desire to hunt; the use of digital collecting will tap into this 'hunting and collecting' instinct.

The use of digital cameras in this activity requires the teacher to determine the level of skills of the children in using the cameras and managing digital data. It may provide a good opportunity to develop children's skills—for example, in using the camera, downloading and filing images, or creating presentations with them. The teacher must decide which of these skills are reasonable expectations of the children.

This activity also provides an opportunity to encourage the children to use ethical behaviour in caring for the environment and making sure they do not disturb or harm living things.

EPISODE 3

What happens if an animal loses its home?

Class discussion

SCIENCE INQUIRY SKILLS *Predict and discuss*

What would happen to us (children and teacher) if we didn't have a home? What would happen to an animal that lost its home? Ask for specific examples, such as what would happen if a bird lost its nest. How might a bird lose its nest? (Here the discussion can be led to habitat loss and the impact of humans—for example, cutting down trees and pollution of air and water.) Perhaps children will suggest some natural causes of habitat loss (e.g. bushfire, flood, storms). Photographs such as that in Figure 4.3 can be useful discussion starters.

Figure 4.3 What would happen if this duck's nest were disturbed? What would happen if many nests in the same area were disturbed?

Teaching point: The questioning helps promote discussion and hypothesising. It also helps children to make connections with prior knowledge or their own experiences and ideas.

The school librarian will be able to suggest reading resources that touch on this theme—for example, *The Great Possum Creek Bush Fire* by Dan Vallely. Such materials allow teachers to make literacy links and provide stimulus for the children's ideas.

Viewing

SCIENCE INQUIRY SKILLS *Observe and discuss*

Watch a documentary about habitat loss or the plight of various animals as their environment is encroached upon—for example, orang-utans or polar bears. Before the viewing, find out what children already know about the particular animals and their habitats. Perhaps select documentaries to watch, some with a focus on animals with which the children are familiar and some with which they are not.

> **Teaching point:** The teacher should always preview documentaries for content suitability. Selecting documentaries about familiar and unfamiliar animals taps into what children already know, and also scaffolds and extends their knowledge into new areas. The school librarian will always help with ideas about where to source appropriate video and book resources. Many teachers also subscribe to online discussion boards, where they can ask colleagues for ideas.

Role-play

SCIENCE INQUIRY SKILLS *Represent and communicate by role-play*

Children can pretend to be various animals, arriving at their home, living in their home and leaving their home. The children can be provided with resources to create a dramatic play area. Around this activity, there is opportunity for development of props through art and craft that will use the children's observations in their creation. While children are in their 'animal homes', present scenarios to help them determine the value of the home—for example, pretend it is raining or very hot or very cold, or that a predator is approaching. Also explore what might happen if the habitat in which they live is altered through human interference.

> **Teaching point:** Role-play is a powerful activity for children. It calls on their imagination and creativity as well as their understandings of the scenario. It also helps develop children's empathy.

Whenever children are involved in art and craft and construction activities, there is a practical application of mathematical concepts associated with measurement or space.

EPISODE 4

Making animal homes

SCIENTIFIC LITERACY *Information can be re-represented using many modes.*

In this episode, data collected as text and image is re-represented through physical and verbal modes.

Research

SCIENCE INQUIRY SKILLS *Research and communicate*

Children in groups with the help of teachers/parents or older children research/discuss an animal of their choice via the library, internet or other gathered resources. Direct the children's choices to animals that have distinct homes or habitats. Children gather information to share with the class using images and/or words. Use the information learned to guide the following activity.

Construction or drawing

SCIENCE INQUIRY SKILLS *Represent ideas*

Children work in small groups. Choose an animal and its corresponding home to represent through drawing or construction. Construction can include various media, such as cloth, clay, play-dough, cardboard and paints.

Presentation

SCIENCE INQUIRY SKILLS *Process and present information*

In groups, children present their representations to the class and explain what the animal is, discuss its home, where the animal might live, how the home protects the animal and how the animal might be threatened if its environment is changed. Children can do this as an oral report or they can act out a scenario.

> **Teaching point:** This culminating activity can be video-recorded and added to the children's digital portfolio and used for assessment purposes.

EXTENSION IDEAS FOR ANIMAL HOMES

Examples of homes where two organisms benefit could be discussed. For example:

- *The shrimp and the goby fish:* The shrimp digs a burrow in the sand, in which both animals live. In return for being able to shelter in the shrimp's burrow, the fish warns the shrimp (which is almost blind) when danger is coming.
- *The gall acacia tree and acacia ants:* The ants live in the galls (bulbous fruits) of the tree. As shown in Figure 4.4, when an animal tries to eat the leaves, the ants defend the tree and protect its leaves from being eaten by animals such as elephants and giraffes.

Figure 4.4 Gall acacia and acacia ants

- Children may like to find out about examples of animals that live together in homes—for example, social weaverbirds, bees, ants or termites. The nests of weaverbirds, termites and hornets are shown in Figure 4.5.

Figure 4.5 Communal homes of (a) weaverbirds, (b) termites, and (c) hornets

BIOLOGICAL SCIENCE   43

BIOLOGICAL SCIENCE 2 ─────────────────

Colour in nature

- **Science understanding**: Living things have observable external features, including colour. They have basic needs, such as protection, which may be gained through the use of colour. Living things may have particular colours that allow them to function in their environments, or they may rely on colour in their homes or habitats.
- **Nature of science**: Explore and observe the use of colour in nature by using senses; observe and question how living things may use colour to their advantage.

OVERVIEW

Living things have many behavioural and structural adaptations that enable them to increase their chances of survival. One example of physical adaptation is colour, which can assist in concealing organisms from predators (camouflage), act as a warning to others (as in the case of toxic animals or plants) or be used as a means of attracting other organisms (think of flowers and bees; male birds attracting females). This unit explores colour in nature with a focus on colour adaptations that help animals or plants through camouflage and high visibility.

EPISODE I ···

Where is it?

Focus activity

SCIENCE INQUIRY SKILLS *Experiment and observe*

Use string to delineate a 4m² area in a grassy place in the school grounds. Make sets of dyed matchsticks (sticks, not matches) using red, green, yellow, and blue food colouring. For each activity 10 sticks of each colour will be needed. Place the sticks into a container and shake. Cast the matchsticks over the 4m². In groups of three, the children will be given one minute in which to collect as many sticks as they can. The groups take turns doing the activity while the other children sit nearby to watch.

> **Teaching point:** This activity allows teachers to reinforce children's skills in counting to ten. It also provides an opportunity to develop children's understanding of time units and their length (in this case, one minute).

Data gathering

SCIENCE INQUIRY SKILLS *Collect, record and represent information*
SCIENTIFIC LITERACY *Scientists represent numerical data using tables and graphs*

After one minute, count the sticks the children have found into colour piles. In this activity, it is usually the green sticks that prove hardest to find. Repeat the activity with other groups, if necessary moving the square to new locations. Continue to count the coloured piles at the end of each group's turn, then collate the data to be displayed on a large graph for the class to see on their return to class.

> **Teaching point:** Doing the activity in this way requires some children to sit quietly and watch others perform the activity (if only for a brief time). This in itself is an important skill for children to develop, especially in science where observation is a key aspect.

This experiment should lead children to start making some general observations that can be tested when data are collected and displayed. It can lead to a 'problem approach' to further learning about colour—for example, why are some colours hard to see and others not? What role does background have to play? How do animals and humans use colour?

This activity lends itself to the development of some mathematical concepts related to statistics and probability. Mathematical language of comparison (more, less, bigger, smaller) could be developed here.

Discussion

SCIENCE INQUIRY SKILLS *Respond, predict, and conclude*

Assuming data show that the green sticks are hardest to find, ask the children questions such as: Which coloured sticks were found most often? Which were found least often? Why is this so? Terms such as 'camouflage' and 'highly visible' can be introduced at some point during this discussion. Develop a word wall.

> **Teaching point:** Notice that the questions progress from factual closed questions to questions that are more probing, requiring children to reason or elaborate. This is a great opportunity for children to experience the power of data to explain a phenomenon. It also allows them to hypothesise. Creating a word wall is a great way to scaffold children's literacy development. They can be encouraged to use the words from the wall and add words to the wall as they learn them. Again this could be done using an IWB.

Discussions such as this provide an excellent opportunity to gather assessment data through annotation, observation or checklisting.

Extension

SCIENCE INQUIRY SKILLS *Explore, manipulate, and work as a team to solve a problem, predict*

Different groups can conduct the same matchstick activity in a number of ways. Children can conduct activities with help where needed. They can then report back to the class using data tables or graphic representations. Examples of variations include the following:

- The location of the square can be moved to different coloured surfaces (e.g. an area of dry grass, a leaf-covered area) to determine whether the colour of the background affects the locating of the sticks.
- Specific colours can be allocated to particular children, and they can be timed to see how long it takes to locate certain colours.

Teaching point: These variations can be used for developing numeracy skills by authentic engagement in data collection, comparison of data, measuring time, counting and adding. The skills and concepts associated with these aspects may need to be explicitly taught or revised. Student products would be useful for assessment for learning purposes.

EPISODE 2

Lost and found

Visual activity

SCIENCE INQUIRY SKILLS *Observe, classify, predict and hypothesise*
SCIENTIFIC LITERACY   *Development of scientific terminology*

Show the class a slide show of images such as those in Figure 4.6, depicting the use of colour to stand out from the environment or to blend in with the environment (camouflage). These can be pictures of plants and animals as well as humans that wish to be easily seen or not easily seen. Let children decide whether the image depicts camouflage or high visibility. Ask questions such as: Why would someone or something try to be seen or not seen?

Teaching point: Again notice how questioning is used to extend children's reasoning. The shared responses help all children to develop a deeper understanding of the concepts.

Figure 4.6 In these images, (a) the buttercup flower, (b) Heuglin's courser (birds), (c) the caracal (a type of African cat) and (d) the sidewinder adder use colour to their advantage. How do they do this?

BIOLOGICAL SCIENCE   47

Painting

SCIENCE INQUIRY SKILLS *Experiment, share and explain*

Children in pairs choose from an assortment of plastic model creatures. Their task is to paint two different backgrounds for the creature. One background is to use colours that will make the creature difficult to see and the other is to make the creature easy to see (see Figure 4.7). Backgrounds to paint can be shoeboxes or simply A4 paper or similar folded in half, with one half being the ground surface and the other half being the background. At the end of the task, children can share their efforts with the class and explain why they chose their backgrounds and colours for camouflage and easy visibility.

Figure 4.7 This illustration shows how the same plastic creature (warthog) can seem to change colour depending on its background. It looks darker against the light background on the left (a), and lighter against the dark background on the right (b).

Teaching point: Children could try similar experiments of colour contrast using varied backgrounds and different coloured clothing. Record the result with a digital camera.

Recording the children's responses to the question of their choice of colours in their products can contribute to assessment evidence.

Extending the discussion

SCIENCE INQUIRY SKILLS *Predict and discuss*

Ask why it is sometimes important for humans to be seen—for instance, road safety, at night time or in a hazardous workplace. What can be done to make the person safer through increasing visibility?

48 TEACHING EARLY YEARS MATHEMATICS, SCIENCE AND ICT

> **Teaching point:** Here perhaps the children go beyond what they know, but this is an opportunity for them to apply what they have learnt to new situations. The teacher's questioning provides a structure that scaffolds the children to do this.

EPISODE 3

Why are many flowers so colourful?

Field trip

SCIENCE INQUIRY SKILLS *Explore, collect using digital technologies and represent ideas*

In the school environment or a nearby park, conduct a flower hunt. Take photos of as many types and colours of flowers as possible. If flowers aren't available, then perhaps ask the children to bring some from home to place around the classroom. Count how many different colours of flowers are found or collected, and record on a colour chart and word wall.

> **Teaching point:** Recording of photos and data provides an opportunity to develop children's ICT skills. The children's scientific vocabulary can be increased by learning the names of some simple flower parts (such as petals or stamens). In addition, the activity can be useful for developing or revising the children's mathematical skills related to counting, number comparison and data representation.

Discussion

SCIENCE INQUIRY SKILLS *Predict and discuss*

While viewing the flowers or photos of flowers, ask children why they think flowers are so often brightly coloured (see Figure 4.8). Did they notice any insect or bird life near the flowers?

> **Teaching point:** The final question here is an example of focusing children's attention on a particular aspect that the teacher wishes to emphasise. Other questions encourage reasoning. The discussion can obviously move to the notion of the flowers' method of reproduction or insects' and birds' collection of nutrition. Teachers should use their judgement as to whether to pursue this further.

BIOLOGICAL SCIENCE   49

Figure 4.8 How does the colour of the flower help both the bee and the flower?

Drawing, painting and labelling

SCIENCE INQUIRY SKILLS *Use language and represent ideas*

Children create a flower wall with drawings and paintings of their own flower creations. Alternatively, children can create flowers out of coloured paper through paper cutting and folding. Use words with which they have become familiar during the unit to label the flowers and colours. Ask children to write (with or without adult help) a brief statement about their flower, its colour and its purpose.

> **Teaching point:** This is a great opportunity for children to learn the names of some of the flowers and their colours. It is also possible to introduce nuances of colour, such as light pink or dark red.

The children's responses can be collected and used in an assessment portfolio.

EXTENSION IDEAS

- Children could think about questions such as: Have you ever seen a green flower? Why do you think many plants have flowers that are not green?
- Differences between feather colours of male and female birds can be an interesting topic to discuss. The male bird is often very brightly coloured while the female is often coloured to blend in with the habitat, as shown in Figure 4.9. This use of colour can be linked to ideas about protecting animals or their young. What would happen if the female bird was brightly coloured? Would it be easy for her to keep the location of the nest secret from predators? Why are some male birds brightly coloured?

Figure 4.9 In this illustration, the male king parrot in the foreground is more brightly coloured than the female in the background

- Colours of some fish help them to avoid predators—for example, some reef fish have a false eye on their tail-end. Why might this help the fish survive? Some fish have stripes, which can cause visual disruption to the predator—how could this help the fish survive? Find online images.
- Some animals—for example, praying mantis and leaf insects—have the same structure as parts of their environment (e.g. they are shaped like twigs or leaves). How might this help them survive? Find online images.

Teaching point: In each of these extension ideas, the children have been asked some hypothetical questions requiring them to apply existing knowledge to a hypothetical situation.

Planning and reflection

Use the Planning and Reflection for Teaching template in Chapter 1 to more deeply consider and make personal decisions about the pedagogy, curriculum and assessment possibilities or requirements for this unit.

Chemical science

Chemical science focuses on understanding matter—how it is structured, its properties, how these relate to each other and how materials can be modified for particular purposes. In this topic, we also seek to understand the ways in which different substances react with one another and the products of these reactions. This is an area of science that is notoriously difficult for many students, particularly as they advance through school, because much of our understanding of the chemical world relies on models and symbols to represent things that we can't see (such as atoms, molecules and reactions). In the early grades, the important understandings relate to children knowing that different substances and materials are structured in different ways, and that this can affect how they behave, and consequently what we use them for. In this topic, the children explore mixtures and the properties of different mixtures and their components to start developing their skills of observation and their understanding of the links between properties and uses. At this level, the properties and structures discussed are all observable.

Integration of mathematics and ICT into chemical science

In this chapter, the integration of mathematics and ICT includes, but is not limited to:

- *Number and Algebra:* practical use of numbers in recipes and measuring temperature and time
- *Geometry and Measurement:* naming some 3D shapes; exploring capacity by comparing equal or proportional amounts in recipes; mixing, measuring and manipulating quantities using formal and/or informal units; basic use of temperature to make freezing temperature comparisons; informally comparing time intervals
- *Statistics and Probability:* data collection and representation in tables
- *ICT:* digital cameras to capture images for making picture books and claymations; IWB for collating, displaying and viewing; viewing of video clips of stimulus books; using digital microscopes; internet for online searches to investigate and gather information on videos and artwork, colour-by-number websites, and searching for recipes and experiments; software and apps as appropriate.

CHEMICAL SCIENCE 1 ─────────────────────────

Mixing it

- **Science understanding**: Materials have properties such as colour, texture, smell and temperature, which may be observed using the senses. Some of these materials can be changed through mixing with other materials.
- **Nature of science**: Science knowledge helps people to control the changes that occur when materials are mixed. It also allows people to make mixtures for particular purposes.

OVERVIEW

In this unit, children will be guided through explorations of the properties of various materials and the changes that occur when they are mixed in various ways. The properties of the materials will be observed and described before and after they are mixed. Children will be asked to describe how mixing materials can change or improve them for a particular purpose. In the first episode, the approach is guided play, whereas in the final episode, the approach involves demonstration and guided exploration. This episode provides an opportunity for the children to practise following simple procedures—an important scientific skill.

54 TEACHING EARLY YEARS MATHEMATICS, SCIENCE AND ICT

EPISODE 1 ··

An unusual mix

Focus demonstration activity

SCIENCE INQUIRY SKILLS *Describe, predict, experiment and reason*

Resources: A transparent demonstration container (plastic or glass beaker), equal amounts of water and corn starch (e.g. a cup of water and a cup of corn starch), several separate sample containers (plastic cups) containing equal quantities of water and corn starch, and stirring sticks for children's experiments and observations.

Activity: Ensure that each group of children has access to a small container of water and a small container of corn starch (variously called corn starch or cornflour in some countries). Ask children to describe the water and record their responses, then repeat the questioning for corn starch.

Ensure their responses reflect the use of multiple senses, not just sight. What does it feel like, smell like, behave like?

Ask children to predict what they think will happen when the two materials are mixed. Will the resulting mixture have any properties of the original materials? In what ways do they think things will change by mixing?

Conduct a front-of-class demonstration using the transparent container and the water and corn starch (the more of each the better for this demonstration). Put the water in the container and then slowly add and stir the corn starch. (The stirring will become progressively more difficult as more corn starch is added. Gentle slow stirring will work best.) Emphasise that the two materials are being mixed and that they are changing in various ways. Ask children to describe what is happening visually.

When the mixing is complete, the mixture should behave in an unusual way. Using the transparent container to demonstrate, slowly push a finger into the mixture (it should move into the mixture), then quickly push or jab a finger into the mixture (the mixture should resist the push), as seen in Figure 5.1. Ask the children to move to the demonstration area, then repeat the activity with their participation.

> **Teaching point:** This experiment should lead children to start making some general observations about mixing. The two materials have combined and the new mixture demonstrates different properties from those of the original materials. These ideas are facilitated through the use of questions that require prediction and observation. Encourage good 'science experiment' behaviour, such as following instructions and being safe with materials.

CHEMICAL SCIENCE   55

Figure 5.1 When enough corn starch has been added to the water, the mixture becomes very thick and behaves differently when a finger is slowly immersed than when it is jabbed at the mixture

Making this mixture is a little difficult, so teachers should try it at home first to decide whether they feel their class could make the mixture or whether this activity is best left as a demonstration or managed by giving the children pre-mixed containers. If you decide to proceed with children mixing these ingredients, allow them to play with the resulting mixture, trying to push objects into the mixture quickly and slowly and observing the difference.

There is some opportunity to develop mathematical ideas such as estimating and making equal quantities.

Viewing

SCIENCE INQUIRY SKILLS *Observe, discuss and reason*

Search online for some great videos clips of large-scale demonstrations of this corn starch and water experiment using a small pool. People can walk quickly across the mixture, but if they stop, they sink into it. These videos are great for further discussion, and allow children to gain an insight into an experience not available in the classroom.

Discussion

SCIENCE INQUIRY SKILLS *Respond to questions and draw conclusions*
SCIENTIFIC LITERACY   *Developing new science vocabulary*

Emphasising the word 'properties', ask children to describe the properties of the corn starch and water mixture. What seemed/felt unusual about this mixture? What action was needed to create the mixture (stirring)? Develop a word wall. Reiterate the notion that, by mixing, the properties of the two original materials have changed, and that the mixture that has been formed has some different properties. How do they think this may have occurred? Are there other situations where mixing two (or more) materials produces something new (e.g. cooking, making play dough).

> **Teaching point:** The unusual properties of the corn starch and water mixture have an interesting analogy. The mixture behaves similarly to a crowd of people: If one tries to run quickly into a crowd of people, progress is rapidly slowed or stopped because the people cannot move out of the way quickly enough. However, if one walks slowly into the crowd, then progress is possible because people can move around you.

EPISODE 2 ··

Mixing colours

Creating a paint chart

SCIENCE INQUIRY SKILLS *Observe, experiment and reason*

During art/painting activities, ask children to see whether they can make new or different colours to the ones on their paint palettes—perhaps begin with just three colours. Try to emphasise the idea of mixing. Let the children explore the various combinations and the new colours they make.

Later, ask the children whether anyone knows how to make certain colours by mixing others—for example, they may know that to make green they need to mix blue and yellow.

Prepare blank colour charts similar to that shown in Figure 5.2. The children are to put a dab of differently coloured paint in each of the first two boxes of each row and then mix the two (on their palettes) to give the new colour for the third box. In between each colour, the children will need to wash out their brushes. Why? (To prevent unintentional mixing.) Transfer the result to the colour chart. Guide the children through the first few examples of mixing. Ask that they try to have the same amount of colour in each of the first two boxes. (Why?)

CHEMICAL SCIENCE   57

Figure 5.2   Sample colour chart

First colour	Second colour	New colour from mixing
 Colour:	 Colour:	 New colour:
 Colour:	 Colour:	 New colour:

Let the children add further rows to the colour chart with their own colour choices. Ask them to predict and name their resulting colours if possible. As an extension to this, encourage children to use different amounts of colour (different ratios) to see what happens to the resulting mix. Does the new mix get lighter, darker, stay the same? Try some experiments making different shades of a colour by mixing in white or black. Emphasise that mixing the colours changes the properties of the original materials (in this case, colour). Relate their observations to what happened to the properties of the original materials in the corn starch and water experiment.

Teaching point: When children are working with only two colours, they can change the resulting colour by varying the relative amounts of the two colours used. Once the children have observed this, they may be able to predict whether their final colour will be lighter or darker, depending on the relative amounts of colour used. While this activity doesn't involve measurement or a known quantity for each of the paints, the children can be engaged in the mathematical concepts of ratio, manipulating one amount relative to the other, and ideas about comparison.

58 TEACHING EARLY YEARS MATHEMATICS, SCIENCE AND ICT

Search online for some examples of great works of art; Monet is good for this activity. Project them on the IWB. Have children try to name the colours used or explain how the artist may have created the colours used. Perhaps have children try to emulate the colours. There are some great 'colour-by-numbers' websites that will allow children to experiment with their new-found colour mixing skills. Continue to draw out the idea that substances' properties (in this case, colour) are being manipulated as the substances are mixed to create a desired outcome.

> **Teaching point:** Literacy links can be made through the many children's books that focus on colour. For example, Leo Lionni's books *Little Blue, Little Yellow* and *A Colour of His Own* may make interesting follow-up readings, or may provide opportunities to introduce and engage the children in this topic. They are also available online as YouTube clips. Perhaps children could use their new colour knowledge combined with ICT skills to create their own picture books or digital claymation stories involving colour.

EPISODE 3

Making ice cream

Experiment

SCIENCE INQUIRY SKILLS *Experiment, collect data and reason*

Resources: Zip-lock plastic bags (big and small), sugar, salt, whipping cream, milk, ice, bowls or cups, spoons.
Demonstration: Conduct a teacher-led front-of-class demonstration to introduce this activity. During this demonstration, take the time to draw out important concepts. Discuss the properties of the ingredients before mixing and what the children predict might happen when the ingredients are mixed. Numerous different recipes for making ice cream are available on the internet.

In a large zip-lock bag, place ice and salt according to the recipe you are following. In a smaller zip-lock bag, put in the desired measures of cream/milk, sugar, optional flavouring (e.g., vanilla). Cream thickens faster than milk, reducing the time taken for the ice cream to form. This may be more desirable for use with young children. Place the smaller bag inside the larger one, seal both, and shake until the mixture begins to freeze (this takes a few minutes).

> **Teaching point:** Completing the teacher-led demonstration and discussion before children attempt the experiment is important, as the activity is quite noisy. It takes quite

CHEMICAL SCIENCE 59

a few minutes of constant shaking of the bags to complete, and children will be focussed on the outcome, so keep discussion and questioning to before and after. Consider the dietary circumstances of children before the children conduct the experiment to perhaps adjust the mixture to suit any special requirements.

Children can now replicate the experiment in small groups (perhaps with adult assistance). The shaking of the bags takes some time and effort, so working in groups will allow for the bags to be passed from child to child to maintain the shaking and mixing. When the ice cream forms, the children could do a taste test. If the flavour is not to their liking (e.g. too sweet, not sweet enough), discuss what might need to be changed in the mixture to create the desired outcome. This will give an opportunity to again discuss the various properties that materials have, and the influence they might have on the properties of the final mixture—for example, the ice and salt caused the other ingredients to freeze by changing their temperature; the sugar or vanilla gave the ice cream mixture a flavour.

Teaching point: This episode provides opportunities to engage children in a number of mathematical ideas, such as measurement, comparison of quantities and estimation.

Measuring

SCIENCE INQUIRY SKILLS *Experimenting and reasoning*

A nice experiment is using a digital thermometer to measure and compare the temperatures of a bag of ice, and a bag of ice and salt. Children should see that the ice and salt mixture is colder than the plain ice. So mixing the ice and salt has created a mixture that allows for the freezing of the ice cream mixture.

Teaching point: This type of activity has the potential for lots of measuring. If your particular cohort is ready for measuring activities (formal or informal), then take the opportunity to have children help in the preparation of materials for the experiment. It also provides the opportunity to introduce the children to different measuring tools (e.g. measuring cups, spoons, thermometer), and even to some units of measurement.

EXTENSION IDEAS

The following activities are suitable for further exploration of mixing materials in various ways to control the final product.

- *Mix water and salt.* Watch what happens to the salt as it is mixed. Place the mixture on a shallow plate or tray, and place in the sun for a period of time. This length of time may vary depending on the intensity of the sun or depth of water. It should be long enough to permit observation of the mixture during and after evaporation. As the water evaporates, the salt will remain. The mixing process has been reversed.

Teaching point: Children may say that the salt has 'disappeared' when mixed with water. The salt particles are still present when mixed, but are too small to be seen because the salt was dissolved. Evaporating the water will show the children that the salt is in fact still present.

- *Conduct a field trip around the classroom and school*, recording materials that have been created by mixing other materials—for example, concrete. Ask the children whether they know what the original materials used in the mix might have been.
- *Collect a small amount of soil and place in a jar with water.* Seal, shake and then allow the contents to settle. Watch the outcome: as the mixture settles, layers of different materials may form.
- *Mix food products* using a recipe—for example, make cordial and water ice blocks, mint and yogurt dip, salsa, or fruit salad. Always draw out the purpose and benefits of mixing, looking at what each ingredient might contribute to the mixture and how the ingredients and quantities need to be considered and controlled.
- *Conduct simple cooking activities*, such as making pancakes, mixing the batter and then using heat to change the state of the mixture. This sequence is shown in Figure 5.3.

Figure 5.3 (a) Initial ingredients for pancakes (recipes available on the internet), (b) the resulting mixture, (c) the change that occurs to the mixture through heating and (d) the final product

CHEMICAL SCIENCE 61

Teaching point: Whenever dealing with recipes, it is important that the quantities of ingredients remain in the same ratio. These activities provide opportunities to talk with children about ratio-related ideas. For example, if our pancakes have one egg and two cups of flour to feed three people, how much of each ingredient would we need to feed six people?

CHEMICAL SCIENCE 2

Bubbles

- **Science understanding:** Bubbles have observable properties, which can be changed in some way. Bubble media (mixtures) can be mixed in different ways; bubbles can be observed in nature; different materials can be combined in different ways for different purposes (in this case, water and soap); and different mixtures may behave in different ways (this may be evident when the children experiment with different bubble media).
- **Nature of science:** Exploring and observing bubbles using the senses, describing changes in bubbles.

OVERVIEW

In this unit, children are given the opportunity to play with bubbles. The teaching approach is guided play, whereby children play and explore during an activity selected and prepared by the teacher. The play and exploration are used as a starting point for further investigations.

62 TEACHING EARLY YEARS MATHEMATICS, SCIENCE AND ICT

EPISODE 1

Making bubbles

Exploring

SCIENCE INQUIRY SKILLS *Explore and communicate*

In an outdoor wet area, provide plastic dishes with dishwashing liquid/bubble medium and various bubble-creating instruments—for example, small circular bubble blowers or larger circular instruments requiring waving to produce bubbles. Bubble media recipes are available on the internet. At this stage, allow the children to engage in the sheer joy of making bubbles. Talk to the children as they play and listen and watch for ideas upon which you could build in future lessons.

> **Teaching point:** Bubble media are like recipes: they require some tweaking to get them just right. So some experimenting on the correct formula can be conducted by the teacher or in conjunction with children as an investigation. Alternatively, bubble media can be purchased at a toy shop or ordered online.

The children might be directed to share what they noticed while exploring the process of making bubbles. For example, what did they notice about the shape, colour or size of the bubbles? How did the bubbles behave (e.g. floating, landing, bursting)? How did they make the bubbles bigger? (The probing nature of this last question is intended to help the children to think about what is inside a bubble.)

If possible, also provide some 3D-shaped bubble instruments—for example, a cube or triangular prism such as those shown in Figure 5.5. These can be made using firm wire such as that from a coathanger and/or connector sticks. The 3D shapes make for some very interesting bubble creations.

EPISODE 2

Inside a bubble

Activity

SCIENCE INQUIRY SKILLS *Experience, explore and observe*

Resources: A large circular tub, some bricks, a plastic hoop (smaller diameter than the tub) and a large quantity of bubble medium.

CHEMICAL SCIENCE 63

Figure 5.4 Some experimenting is needed to develop a good bubble medium

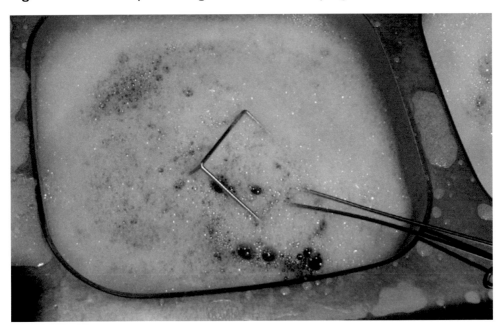

Figure 5.5 Three-dimensional bubble-makers: (a) cube and (b) triangular prism

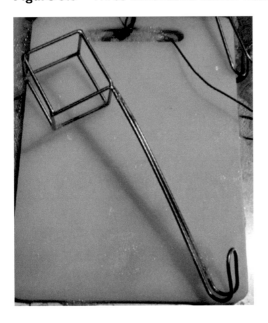 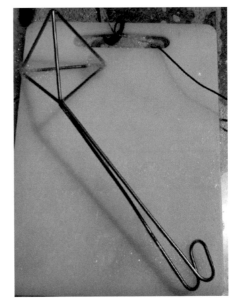

TEACHING EARLY YEARS MATHEMATICS, SCIENCE AND ICT

Set-up: Place the bubble medium in the tub, then place the bricks in the centre to form an island. Place the hoop in the bubble medium in the tub. The set-up is shown in Figure 5.6. *Activity:* There are a number of ways in which children can now engage in this activity. A digital camera can record the children's experiences.

- The child can stand outside the tub and lift the hoop vertically out of the medium, creating a large cylindrical soap-film shape as shown in Figure 5.7. (This is not really a bubble, because the top of the shape around the hoop is not enclosed.)
- The child can step into the tub and lift the hoop as shown in Figure 5.8. The cylindrical soap film surrounds them.
- The child steps into the tub and an adult or classmate can lift the hoop above the child's head. For a few moments the child will be inside the cylindrical 'bubble' as shown in Figure 5.9.

This activity requires some experimentation by the teacher and children to create an effective bubble medium. There are numerous websites available to assist with the formula for the bubble medium. It might be useful to include the children in the experimentation—to think about what happens if there is too much of one component—such as water—in the mixture.

> **Teaching point:** Children will enjoy doing this activity, but they will also enjoy observing it as it is inherently interesting and exciting, and each time the hoop is lifted the size and shape of the soap film will vary.

Discussing, drawing and writing

SCIENCE INQUIRY SKILLS *Respond to questions, develop language, reason and represent*
SCIENTIFIC LITERACY *Vocabulary to describe mixtures, components and properties*

Children are then brought together to share their experiences. What was it like to be inside the soap film? What did they see or feel? What colours did they see? Could they see through the soap film? What happened when the soap film burst? Ask children to describe the soap film: try to elicit ideas of strength, fragility, elasticity, dampness or transparency. Help children to develop language that aids their descriptions of their experiences.

Children can draw pictures of their experience inside the soap film. Display these with labels using new words learned through the experience. The children can also view their experiences from the digital camera on the IWB.

> **Teaching point:** Questioning here elicits thinking and articulation about what children have experienced. This is a nice activity to help the children make the link that our observations are the result of using our senses during experiences.

CHEMICAL SCIENCE   65

Figure 5.6   The bubble tub, bubble medium, island of bricks and hoop

Figure 5.7   Child creating the soap film shape by standing outside

66 TEACHING EARLY YEARS MATHEMATICS, SCIENCE AND ICT

Figure 5.8   The child creates the soap film from within the tub

Figure 5.9   A child inside a soap film created by an adult

CHEMICAL SCIENCE 67

EPISODE **3** ···

Bubbles in everyday life

Research and collecting

SCIENCE INQUIRY SKILLS *Collect, research, observe and reason*

Over time, collect examples of bubbles and bubbling. This can be from internet sources, or videos and digital photos of bubbles and bubbling around the school environment. Images can range from small bubbles formed when a tap is run into a sink, someone blowing bubbles through a straw or bubbles formed when something is cooking in the school canteen. What do bubbles have in common? Can bubbles be different—for example, size, shape, colour, medium and longevity? Look for bubbles in food—for example, bread, cake, chocolate, cheese or froth on milkshakes.

Teaching point: Questioning here requires children to make comparisons and articulate observations. It helps to focus their attention and promote reasoning.

Use a digital microscope to examine other objects that have bubbles—for instance, certain types of rocks, foods or foam. Images such as those shown in Figure 5.10 can also be recorded and used for discussion.

EXTENSION IDEAS

- Bubbles are needed in some cooking—for example, in bread, cakes and chocolate mousse. Children can use magnifying glasses or digital microscopes to look closely at some foods.
- Bubbles, or structures like bubbles, make materials useful for a range of purposes, such as foam in cushions or bubble wrap in packaging. The children can collect materials that use air pockets to make them useful. Perhaps a class discussion would help the children describe the properties that are given to materials because of bubbles or air pockets (e.g. softness, resistance to impact).
- Experiments such as putting yeast with sugar or flour in some tepid water and observing the production of gas can be useful for showing how foods such as bread are made soft and airy. There are many fun experiments online that use yeast, such as *elephant's toothpaste*. Great bubbles are formed when Mentos peppermints are placed in Coca-Cola, which would be fun and engaging demonstrations for an adult to do with the children. Note that while these demonstrations are exciting, they can also be quite messy.

Figure 5.10 Examples of bubbles: (a) in cheese, (b) a crab blowing bubbles and (c) bubbles on a straw

Planning and reflection

Use the Planning and Reflection for Teaching template in Chapter 1 to more deeply consider and make personal decisions about the pedagogy, curriculum and assessment possibilities or requirements for this unit.

Earth and space science

This is a diverse area of science because it encompasses global and local phenomena, such as environment, climate, weather and seasons; changes to the earth, such as earthquakes, weathering and erosion; and astronomical ideas, such as the earth's place in space. Once again, it is not the intention here to suggest that children be exposed to all of these complex ideas, but rather to establish the children's ability to observe changes around them, and to get them to wonder and question why they may occur. The activities in this section lend themselves to connections with other content areas, such as biology and chemistry, which are often needed to either understand geological or environmental phenomena or to appreciate how these phenomena impact on living things.

Integration of mathematics and ICT into earth and space science

In this chapter, the integration of mathematics and ICT includes, but is not limited to:

- *Number and Algebra:* counting and adding
- *Geometry and Measurement:* folding shapes, informal or formal measurement of attributes such as depth and width, cardinal points and directions, simple time/duration concepts, comparisons and an introductory concept of speed

- *Statistics and Probability:* data-collection, representation of data, reasoning about results of data collection
- *ICT:* digital cameras to capture images, create time-lapse sequences, IWB for representing data, image display, modelling keyword internet searching, showing 'live cam' websites, and to display data from a digital microscope and view online experiments, software and apps as appropriate.

EARTH AND SPACE SCIENCE 1 —————————

Puddles and ponds

- **Science understanding:** Puddles and ponds represent aspects of the earth's water resources. Puddles are temporary watery features of our landscape while ponds are more permanent. Puddles and ponds only form in certain places, which are dependent on particular environmental or geological conditions. The temporary versus permanent nature of water features means they can be used in a range of different ways by a variety of different living things, including humans. As with so many areas in science, it is not always possible to present concepts or topics as belonging solely to one area. This earth and space topic relates closely to biological topics, such as ecosystems, and can also be linked to chemical science ideas such as properties of materials.
- **Nature of science:** Science can help us to understand and care for the watery features of our environment. It can help us understand and describe changes that occur in these watery features. We can use our senses to explore these watery places.

OVERVIEW

Through investigation and experimentation, this unit explores some characteristics of water and the materials needed to create puddles and ponds. Children will investigate why and how puddles form in some places but not in others. They will explore why puddles are usually only temporary. What happens to the puddles? The importance of rainfall can be linked to the use of puddles by living things. By expanding the study to include ponds, the difference between the concepts of permanent and temporary can be highlighted, as can the ways in which this difference affects the use of the water feature by living things. The conditions necessary for puddles or ponds to form (e.g. seasonal changes such as rain, or geological conditions such as clay/indentations in the ground) could also be explored or discussed with the children.

72 TEACHING EARLY YEARS MATHEMATICS, SCIENCE AND ICT

EPISODE 1

Making puddles

Focus activity

SCIENCE INQUIRY SKILLS *Respond to questions, predict, explore by manipulating materials and testing ideas*

Set out small piles of various media such as sand, play dough, clay, foam balls, rice, stones or flour in an outdoor area (perhaps in trays on plastic sheeting). Try to use as many different types of media as possible. Also have available small water containers such as plastic cups or jugs. Children in small groups take turns at the challenge of using one of the various media and water to make a puddle. They must try to manipulate/shape the medium so that a puddle can be formed in it.

> **Teaching point:** Using multiple trials of the same medium by different groups will provide solid data. It is a good example of working scientifically because only one aspect—in this case, the medium—is being manipulated. The benefits of doing this can be discussed with the children.

Before the water is poured into the shaped medium, ask children to predict what they think will happen. Will a puddle form? Will the water flow through the medium and spread across the surrounding surface? Will the puddle last a long time or a short time? Let children work together to explore the challenge and to watch other groups when they attempt to form their puddles. At the end of the activity, prompt the children to consider similarities among the groups' puddle designs. Were most media shaped with higher sides and lower centre areas in an attempt to keep the water inside?

> **Teaching point:** This questioning sequence is designed to help children to think scientifically by making predictions, considering possible outcomes and making comparisons.

Data-gathering

SCIENCE INQUIRY SKILLS *Gather data and record, compare and share results*
SCIENTIFIC LITERACY *Different types of data are represented using tables*

EARTH AND SPACE SCIENCE 73

Use a data table similar to Table 6.1. Place a tick, cross or question mark against the name of each medium, depending on the degree of success at making a puddle. Perhaps gather the data on a pencil and paper chart, then transfer it to the IWB for the class to see.

Table 6.1 Sample puddle data table

Material in container	Yes. We made a puddle. (Tick)	No. We didn't make a puddle. (Cross)	We're not sure if we made a puddle. (?)
Sand			
Play dough			
Rice			
Clay			
Stones			

Teaching point: This table allows the children to make predictions and then compare their predictions with their experimental outcomes. The data table could also be retained as an assessment item for inclusion in a portfolio.

Class discussion

SCIENCE INQUIRY SKILLS *Interpreting data and reasoning*
SCIENTIFIC LITERACY *Data presented in one form can be re-represented (e.g. table to graph)*
Different representations allow us to use or interpret data in different ways

Using the projected data table, guide the children to look for patterns. Which media allowed them to make puddles and which did not? Why do they think some media held the water in a puddle and others did not? Collect responses or key words to summarise children's ideas. Which media seem to allow puddles to be formed? Were there any unusual situations—for example, a puddle that formed but then slowly disappeared? Why did this occur? Were there differences in the data collected? Why or why not?

Relate to puddles in nature/the local environment. What might cause puddles to form in some places but not others? Why might puddles disappear? Why might some puddles disappear faster than others? Links can be made here to environmental conditions, such as position relative to sun/shade, and to soil type—is the soil sandy? Does it contain clay? Are the puddles on a hard surface such as concrete?

74 TEACHING EARLY YEARS MATHEMATICS, SCIENCE AND ICT

> **Teaching point:** This kind of questioning sequence initially helps to guide the children's exploration and then assists them in reasoning about the results. It also helps to focus on anomalies, such as the puddle that formed but then disappeared. In addition, such questioning helps to determine what the children know and reveals any inaccurate perceptions they may have. It also helps lead the children to link the experiment to real-world/authentic scenarios.

Asking children to revisit their predictions and compare them with the outcomes helps to promote a classroom culture of risk-taking and an appreciation that science involves experimentation (in which the expected outcome does not always eventuate).

An opportunity for developing mathematical skills and scientific literacy skills exists if the class data table is converted to a graph. The teacher could lead a discussion about the graph, its structure and how to read it. The discussion could be extended to include a comparison of the usefulness of the two representations for different purposes.

EPISODE 2

Watching puddles

Field trip

SCIENCE INQUIRY SKILLS *Explore, reason and record using digital technologies*
SCIENTIFIC LITERACY *Scientists use drawings to record data*

After the next rainfall, explore the school grounds looking for puddles (if the weather doesn't allow this, perhaps use a hose and sprinkler in various locations around the school). Discuss where the puddles are and where they are not, and the surfaces on which they do and do not gather. Perhaps make multiple trips outside during the day or over several days to examine what happens to the puddles. Children can measure the width, depth and circumference of puddles using formal or informal measuring units; they can draw the shapes of the puddles over time. Digital photos can be taken at regular time intervals (time lapse) to explore what happens to puddles. An example is shown in Figure 6.1.

> **Teaching point:** The teacher has multiple opportunities to engage children in mathematical concepts (e.g. geometry and measurement) in this activity.

The time-lapse digital photos can be projected in sequence and children can offer ideas about what they think has happened to the puddle—for example, they may suggest that the water seeped into the ground, the water was drunk by animals, or perhaps they may

Figure 6.1 The temporary nature of a puddle in three stages: (a) water gathers, (b) slowly the water decreases, (c) only a damp area is left

mention evaporation. Alternatively, the children can draw a three- or four-section cartoon sequence of the puddle over time, and annotate the features, then explain what they think happens to the water. Also record any living thing that uses the puddle and the reason for its use—for example, a bird may drink from it (see Figure 6.2).

Figure 6.2 A puddle can be used by (a) an insect to drink or (b) birds to bathe or drink

Emphasise the concept of 'temporary' and explain that this affects how the puddle is used. What would happen if the 'puddle' were permanent? Would we still call it a puddle? What else might we call a small permanent water feature?

> **Teaching point:** The concepts of 'temporary' and 'permanent' are the focus here. As children investigate the more permanent water feature of a pond, the way the water feature is used by living things will change because of the difference between these two concepts. These ideas can be used to make links to other topics, such as those about habitat.

Using work on puddles as a stimulus, children could engage in numerous literacy activities—for example, writing or telling stories about puddles.

EPISODE 3

From puddle to pond

Research and viewing

SCIENCE INQUIRY SKILLS *Research and compare*

From the previous discussion, children may have offered numerous names for a small permanent water feature—for example, waterhole, pool or pond. If suggestions such as creek, lake and ocean are made, take the opportunity to discuss the differences between these geographic features. Use the children's responses to again emphasise the characteristics of puddles and ponds. In comparing puddles and ponds, characteristics that distinguish them can be used to explain why ponds are permanent and puddles are not—for example, how do they differ in terms of area, depth or location? Seasonal changes could also be linked to the permanency or otherwise of puddles and ponds—for example, how are ponds affected in winter, in summer, during the rainy season, during drought? Children can be asked to make predictions about what they think might happen.

(If there is a pond available in the school or in the local area, then some of what follows may not be needed.) Together, using the internet and IWB, research 'ponds'. Look for examples of ponds and their use by living things. Some examples are shown in Figure 6.3.

Figure 6.3 Because ponds are permanent water features, they can be used by living things in many ways—for example, (a) a bird might find food, (b) a terrapin can live in it, (c) plants can grow and (d) a dog can cool off or have a drink

Teaching point: Here the teacher can model some simple internet research techniques such as 'keywords' and searching for information or images. Ask children for suggestions. There are some great 'live cam' sites that will allow children to view ponds/waterholes being used by creatures.

With guiding questions, focus the children on the permanent nature of ponds, and how this allows living things to rely on them to a greater extent than the temporary puddles. Where possible, emphasise or elicit from the children the need to protect these permanent ponds for the sake of the living things that rely on them.

EPISODE 4

Visiting a pond

Field trip

SCIENCE INQUIRY SKILLS *Observe, collect, reason*

If possible, visit a pond in the local area. Ask children to sit in a safe area nearby and simply use their senses. A number of activities can be completed:

EARTH AND SPACE SCIENCE   79

- Ask children to use their sense of sight to take note of any living things present in and around the pond.
- Ask children to close their eyes and listen for living things in the area.
- Look for living things and signs of living things (animal and plant) that might live in the pond and those that might just visit.
- How do different living things use the pond? For food, drink, breeding (laying eggs), as a habitat (e.g. fish, waterlilies, reeds)?
- Water samples can be collected for microscopic examination back in the classroom.

On your return to class, numerous activities can be undertaken to represent the children's observations. Class lists can be generated of the various living things detected; drawings and paintings can be made of the pond and its inhabitants and surrounds; more in-depth research can be conducted into aspects of pond life. Once again, the focus is on the benefits that result from its permanent nature.

Teaching point: Digital microscopes are available at relatively low cost. These are useful for viewing water samples using the IWB.

EXTENSION IDEAS

Create a class aquarium or school pond. Attending to safety and environmental sensitivities, use research, observations and children's ideas to create a water feature that will allow ongoing classroom learning opportunities.

Such a resource may allow children to observe feeding patterns or behaviour of different organisms. This may permit discussions of simple ecological relationships, such as food chains. This is an example of the interconnection between biological science ideas and environmental/earth science topics.

Children could learn about the ways in which humans use ponds—for example, a farmer may use a pond or dam to breed stock (as in aquaculture), as a permanent water source for animals or as a source of water for irrigation. Perhaps this could involve a guest speaker who describes how ponds are used in their work or leisure activities, or an excursion to allow the children to observe at first hand how ponds are used—for example, by farmers.

80 TEACHING EARLY YEARS MATHEMATICS, SCIENCE AND ICT

EARTH AND SPACE SCIENCE 2 ───────────────────

The wind

- **Science understanding:** Wind (or calm) is a daily part of our environment's weather. It can affect our lives in different ways. The wind can cause observable changes in our environment. It can also be used as one of earth's renewable resources.
- **Nature of science:** The wind can be observed using our senses. Science helps us to understand the wind and how we can use it.

OVERVIEW

In this unit, children explore the wind: what it is and how we can detect it. The notion that wind is the result of convection currents and differences in atmospheric conditions is beyond the scope of science in these grades; however, children can still engage in many activities about the wind. In this unit, the activities involve children developing an understanding of how the wind's direction (including cardinal points) and strength (based on the terminology of the Beaufort Scale) are measured. Children will consider the effects of the wind and how it might be useful (e.g. as a source of energy) or harmful to living things, including humans.

EPISODE 1 ···

Any way the wind blows

Listening and viewing

SCIENCE INQUIRY SKILLS *Observe using senses*

Through questioning, determine the children's understanding of the wind. While inside the room, ask the children whether it is windy or calm outside. How can they tell? If it is windy, perhaps they can see trees swaying or dust blowing, or they might be able to hear some movements caused by the wind. Move outside the classroom and ask the children the same questions. The answers will perhaps include some different responses from when the children were inside. Ask children to close their eyes. Can they still tell whether it is windy or calm? How? Besides using eyes and ears, are there any other ways of deciding whether it is windy or calm? Children may say that they can feel the wind. Draw out the point that we can't **see** the wind—only the **effects** of the wind.

On your return to the classroom, ask children to explain what the wind is. Ask them to try to describe the wind. Think, pair, share could be used to allow the children to consider their explanations individually, with a partner and then as a class group.

EARTH AND SPACE SCIENCE 81

Teaching point: The children's explanations could be collected and revisited at the end of the unit.

Defining the wind can be difficult for children. They may refer to the consequences of wind—for example, objects moving or making noises. Try to elicit that wind is moving air and that its movement creates these other phenomena. How wind is generated is a more complex question. It involves abstract ideas and unobservable phenomena. If you choose to engage the children in this idea, you would need to consider how you would explain such concepts as convection currents and atmospheric pressure. Check websites for possible ideas.

Discussion and role-play

SCIENCE INQUIRY SKILLS *Respond to questions, interpret information*
SCIENTIFIC LITERACY *Scientific terminology associated with wind strength*

Extend the discussion to determine children's knowledge and understanding—for instance, what are some other names for the wind (relate to the varying strengths of wind: breeze)? The Beaufort scale, shown in Table 6.2, can help guide the descriptors of various wind strengths.

Table 6.2 The Beaufort Scale, showing descriptors used to differentiate the strengths of the wind

Calm	0–1 km/h	Light air	2–5 km/h	Light breeze	6–11 km/h
Gentle breeze	12–19 km/h	Moderate breeze	20–28 km/h	Fresh breeze	29–38 km/h
Strong breeze	39–49 km/h	Near gale	50–61 km/h	Gale	62–74 km/h
Strong gale	75–88 km/h	Storm	89–102 km/h	Violent storm	103–117 km/h
Cyclone	118+ km/h				

Teaching point: The speed of the wind on the Beaufort Scale may not be relevant for general use in younger grades of school, although some children will find it interesting—especially as they can relate the wind speed to the speeds of their family car.

> The descriptors such as 'light air' or 'fresh breeze' can be very helpful with children's language and concept development. Inexpensive digital weather stations that include anemometers for recording wind speed are available; these can be set up in the classroom and used for daily weather observations, including wind speed and direction (see Figure 6.4). This presents further opportunities for numeracy development.

Figure 6.4 Inexpensive digital weather stations are now available that use anemometers to give the classroom live information feeds about weather phenomena, including the wind speed

It may be interesting or helpful for the children to collect and display photos from magazines or newspapers depicting the results of varying wind strengths (e.g. storms and cyclones) to match to descriptors on the Beaufort scale—this will help them to visualise the strength of the wind in different situations.

To assist children in their understanding of the concept of relative wind speeds, they could role-play being the wind at different strengths—for example, standing still to represent calm, walking slowing to represent light air, walking quickly to represent a light breeze.

EARTH AND SPACE SCIENCE   83

Classifying activity

SCIENCE INQUIRY SKILLS *Classify and sort information and reason*

Ask the children to name things in their environment that are visibly affected by the wind—for example, leaves rustling, trees swaying and clothes on a line flapping. Using the video function on classroom digital cameras will capture these things nicely, and the images are easy to share on the IWB. Figure 6.5 shows a flag blowing.

Figure 6.5 The wind may cause a flag to move in different ways, depending on the strength and direction of the wind

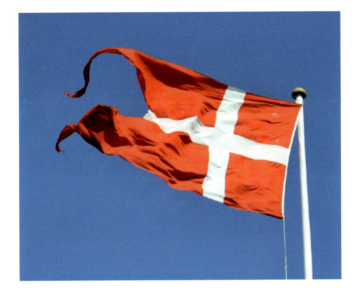

Label hoops or large string circles on the classroom floor as follows:

1. things the wind can't move at all (e.g. classroom)
2. things the wind can move but without changing its location (e.g. a tree can sway), and
3. things the wind can move from one place to another (e.g. dust, papers, leaves).

Give children pictures or word cards of objects that will be affected by the wind in these various ways, then ask them to classify them using the hoops or string circles. If debate arises over some objects belonging to more than one classification, take the opportunity to consider intersecting sets—for example, a tree may sway but not move unless in a very high wind, when it may be blown over.

Teaching point: This is quite an open activity—it is the children's reasoning that is important here when they justify why an object should be positioned in a particular category. This activity provides an authentic way to introduce basic mathematical concepts associated with Venn diagrams.

EPISODE 2

Move with the wind

Drama and language

SCIENCE INQUIRY SKILLS *Communicate through role-play*

SCIENTIFIC LITERACY *Scientific terminology, linking physical phenomena with their verbal representations*

In an open space defined by the cardinal points of north, south, east and west, the children pretend to be various items affected by the wind. The teacher may start with an example but then ask the children to suggest the item, the strength of the wind and the direction from which it blows. First teach the idea that wind is given the name of the direction from which it comes—for example, an easterly breeze comes from the east. All children try to portray the scenario. For example, a child may say that there is a gentle breeze blowing from the east and we are all flags on a pole. As the children describe the scenarios, discuss the words used and collate a word wall—for example, cardinal points, wind words such as breeze and gale, qualifiers such as gentle or strong, and subsequent actions such as rustling, flapping, ruffling, buffeting or swirling.

Teaching point: This is the kind of activity that can be repeated regularly (perhaps during daily weather observations) to help consolidate concepts and language. Literacy activities could be used in which the children practise using the new vocabulary in stories or poems about the wind.

EPISODE 3

Making air move

Construction

SCIENCE INQUIRY SKILLS *Manipulate materials, respond to questions, use senses*

On an A4 sheet of paper, each child can colour or paint a scene of a windy day. Once the artwork is complete, instruct children on how to fold the paper into a fan shape, as shown in Figure 6.6. Allow the children to fan themselves. What do they have to do to make the fan work? When the fan moves, it makes air move. How can they control the speed or direction of the air movement? What effect does the moving air have on them? Does it cool them? Why? Some questions that might help the children's thinking include: What happens if they change the distance between themselves and the fan? How does the speed of fanning affect the air they feel?

Figure 6.6 A paper fan can be used to consider many questions about moving air

As an extension to this activity, have the children take turns at being blindfolded. Ask one or more children to use their fans on the blindfolded person. The blindfolded child must use their sense of touch to decide how many fans are moving air towards them and in what locations.

Children can use the paper fan to attempt to move other objects—for example, to move a feather or small piece of paper across their desk or to cause small objects (e.g. an empty matchbox) to blow over. This will help them to understand the effects of moving air and to develop the ideas that wind speed is related to wind strength and wind is a source of energy.

EPISODE 4

Using the wind

Construction

SCIENCE INQUIRY SKILLS *Manipulate materials, respond to questions, reason*

The idea here is for children to construct a device (or devices) that will use the wind to move. Construction possibilities include:

- a pinwheel
- a mobile of wind pictures or words
- a kite
- a simple foam boat with a paper sail
- a flag
- an anemometer
- a wind sock
- a wind vane.

Detailed instructions for all these devices and more are available on the internet.

At the conclusion of the construction, install as many devices as possible in and around the classroom. Ask children whether the devices behave differently depending on their location, the wind speed, and the wind direction.

> **Teaching point:** This activity provides opportunities across numerous curriculum areas, such as art and craft, mathematics (measurement) and literacy.

Discussion and viewing

SCIENCE INQUIRY SKILLS *Discuss, respond to questions, communicate and reason*

Draw children's attention to the fact that they have constructed devices that react to the presence of the wind. Introduce the idea that this movement of air is a source of energy that can be used by living things, including humans. For example, some plants rely on the wind to disperse their seeds; some birds use the movement of air to help them fly long distances. Ask children whether they can give examples of how humans use the wind. After they have offered some of their ideas, show them some picture examples such as those in Figure 6.7 and ask them to explain what is happening.

EARTH AND SPACE SCIENCE   87

Figure 6.7 Humans have built devices to use the wind's energy: (a) a windmill turns with the wind and pumps water, (b) a sailing boat uses the wind to move and (c) wind turbines use the wind to generate electricity

Experimenting with drying clothes

SCIENCE INQUIRY SKILLS *Experiment, gather data, predict and draw conclusions*

Do our clothes dry better on a windy day? On a windy day, wet two identical tea towels and ask the children to help design an experiment to decide whether the wind helps to dry our clothes. Through questioning, try to elicit ideas from children that the towels could be hung in different places, such as in the shade and wind and in the shade with no wind (inside the classroom). Determine which towel dries fastest. Repeat the experiment and gather data. Display results on a simple graph. Children can make their own graph and, with or without adult assistance, make some statements about the effect of the wind on drying the towels.

Figure 6.8 Clothes drying in the breeze—does the wind help to dry our clothes? How else do people use the wind to their advantage?

Teaching point: This is a good opportunity to ask questions about the design of the investigation such as: Why is it important that both tea towels are in the shade? It is an important aspect of science investigating to change only one variable at a time (in this case, the wind) and keep all others the same. For example, if one towel was in the shade and wind and the other was in the sun with no wind, we wouldn't know which aspect caused one towel to dry faster than the other. Links could be made here to the unit on puddles, in which the idea that the water has gone (evaporated) was introduced. The same thing is happening when the towel dries.

EXTENSION IDEAS
* Investigate the possible harmful effects of wind on living things, including humans, as well as on non-living things.
* There are some good demonstrations on the internet that can be used to show children how (red-coloured) hot water and (blue-coloured) cold water behave when placed in a container of room-temperature water. This can be a nice model to illustrate a similar phenomenon to the one that happens in the air to cause wind (i.e. convection currents caused by differences in temperature); since it is not possible to observe these currents in the air, using coloured water provides a visual example of a similar phenomenon in a liquid. This can be conducted as a demonstration in the classroom with children's assistance.

Planning and reflection

Use the Planning and Reflection for Teaching template in Chapter 1 to more deeply consider and make personal decisions about the pedagogy, curriculum and assessment possibilities or requirements for this unit.

Physical science

Physical science focuses on energy and forces to explain how things move, the forces that cause this movement, sources and forms of energy, and the ways in which energy can be transformed and used for different purposes. Such scientific understanding has great implications for our everyday lives—for example, the use of electricity and transport. It also has implications for technological development. Physical science can help us to understand phenomena that impact on a global scale, from green energy production to nuclear power. As with chemical science, many of the concepts children encounter in physical science are not easily observed and, as a result, children can find it difficult to understand them. In this topic, the activities are designed to allow children to observe the effects of forces on the movement of objects and the outcomes of motion when objects collide. Children can be introduced to simple diagrams to represent motion and force.

Integration of mathematics and ICT into physical science

In this chapter, the integration of mathematics and ICT includes but is not limited to:

- *Number and Algebra:* using and comparing numbers and counting; using Venn diagrams (overlapping sets) for collating data; looking for patterns in data
- *Geometry and Measurement:* comparing attributes such as mass, size, shape; concept of speed (a rate); discussion (but not measurement) of angles

PHYSICAL SCIENCE   91

- *Statistics and Probability:* collecting, displaying and interpreting data; creating data tables
- *ICT:* digital cameras to capture and sequence images; IWB for listing, classifying and viewing, demonstrating online searches and viewing of online materials; digital microscopes; organising and managing files and downloads; use of text display such as Wordle; software and apps as appropriate.

PHYSICAL SCIENCE I

How things move

- **Science understanding:** Objects move in a variety of ways. Humans can cause objects to move by pushing or pulling. Pushes and pulls can start or stop things moving, change their speed if they are already moving or cause them to change direction. Science helps us understand how things move and helps us create objects that move.
- **Nature of science:** Exploring and observing movement using senses. Science involves describing changes in objects and events.

OVERVIEW

This is an investigation into how some things move. It is not possible to consider all aspects of this topic; rather, the aim is to entice children to think about the fact that things—living and non-living—move and are propelled in many ways. It includes discussion about what pushes and pulls are, and where we use them in everyday situations.

EPISODE I

What is movement?

Role-play

SCIENCE INQUIRY SKILLS *Communicate through role-play*

As a focus activity, have the children portray the movement of various common things—for example, a snake, a fly, a car, a truck, a tree, a washing machine. Ask children to give some further suggestions and have the group complete the movements. Now set some parameters for their portrayals—for example, things that move underground, in the sea or in the sky, or only human-manufactured things.

> **Teaching point:** By setting the parameters, the teacher guides the activity but still gives some freedom of ideas to the children. The concepts suggested here may need further investigations—for example, children may not have a clear idea of what 'human-manufactured' means. This would be a great opportunity to find out what the children know and let it guide your planning.

There are some human-made objects that move because they have motors (e.g. cars, fans, planes) and others that move when we push or pull them (e.g. lawnmower, stroller). These will be further explored later in this topic.

Classroom observation

SCIENCE INQUIRY SKILLS *Observe and classify*

This activity can begin inside the classroom but it can also be extended by taking the children outside. As a group, ask the children to name (teacher lists on the IWB) as many things as possible that they can see that:

- are moving
- aren't moving but could move
- could never move.

Then extend to things that:

- move by themselves (independently)
- only move with assistance—by nature (e.g. wind) or by humans (e.g. pushing or pulling).

Make separate lists for each type. Some children may want to place an object in more than one list, which would be a great time to discuss how this might happen. Initially, keep this discussion to what children can see but then expand to things they know—or perhaps prepare a set of images such as those in Figure 7.1 that could be discussed and classified.

EPISODE **2**

How do we make things move? Pushes and pulls

In this episode, the children are shown pictures of objects that are commonly used in our everyday lives or pictures of people using these objects. Figure 7.2 shows some examples. The children are asked to decide whether the movement of the objects involves a push or a pull. Sometimes both answers may be correct.

Figure 7.1 (a) The rocking rabbit moves but like a tree does not change position: (b) a bicycle moves with human power (though it may coast down a hill with the help of gravity)

Movement activity and class discussion

SCIENCE INQUIRY SKILLS   *Answer questions about everyday objects, classify and explain, use representations to sort information (Venn diagrams) and draw to represent ideas (arrows)*

SCIENTIFIC LITERACY   *Some diagrams and symbols are used by scientists to represent things that cannot be seen—for example, arrows to represent the direction of forces*

Introduce this activity by having the children experience the actions of pushing and pulling and by asking them to pretend to complete certain actions. For example, they can pretend to push a stroller or shopping trolley, push or pull a drawer or pull a heavy load. Now give each child a simple object such as a block and ask the children to use the actions of push and pull to move the block away from and towards them.

Using pictures, either on the IWB or on cards, ask the children to identify whether the object or activity involves a push or a pull. Using a Venn diagram (e.g. using string or hoops on the floor with picture cards or pictures on the IWB), sort the actions in the pictures into pushes or pulls. If the children suggest that both actions could be applied to an object or used in an activity, it can go in the common space.

Figure 7.2 (a) A person's wheelchair may be pushed by another person or the user may turn the wheels to make him or her mobile; (b) a wheelbarrow requires a person to make it move: it is usually pushed though it can also be pulled (c) a trailer is usually pulled by a car

> **Teaching point:** The main goal of this activity is to have the children understand what is meant by the terms *push* and *pull*.

If children suggest placing the picture in both the push and pull categories, the key thing is to ask them for an explanation: this encourages children to think about what information they are using to make a claim—a very important scientific skill.

If the children have difficulty identifying push or pull in the pictures, allow them to role-play the pictured activity and describe their actions. Encouraging them to observe someone else can also help.

This activity provides an authentic reason for using Venn diagrams because they solve the problem of classification when some objects can be categorised in more than one way. The use of Venn diagrams provides an opportunity to introduce mathematical ideas associated with sets.

Suggestions of push and pull activities include the following:

- weeding the garden
- picking fruit from a tree
- walking with a stroller
- mowing the lawn
- pressing a button in a lift
- pushing a wheelbarrow
- turning a light switch on and off
- putting the lid on and off a pen
- launching a paper plane
- moving a chair under or away from a desk
- hitting a ball with a bat
- using a clothes peg
- closing or opening a zipper.

Once the children have classified the activities into push, pull or both, lead them in a discussion about how, in all these cases, humans are applying either a push or a pull to make the object move in some way. This will lead to the idea that pushes and pulls influence the way objects move. In addition, the idea that movement sometimes changes the position of part of an object (but not always its overall location—for example, leaves move but a tree stays in position) can be discussed.

On the pictures, mark the direction of the push or pull with an arrow to reinforce the idea that pushes and pulls influence movement in a particular direction. This introduces children to the scientific convention of representing forces and movement using arrows. The arrow indicates direction of the force or movement.

EPISODE 3

Exploring the ways in which things move—using motion words to complete an obstacle course

The goal of this activity is for children to experience the range of ways in which objects can move, and to broaden their vocabulary associated with movement. The activity begins in the classroom by creating a word wall about movement and culminates with the children completing an obstacle course to enact the words they have been using in class.

Talking about moving

SCIENCE INQUIRY SKILLS *Engage in discussion, share ideas*

Ask the children to suggest words that describe how things move. This should include ways of moving (e.g. roll, drop, bounce, slide, fall); ways to make things move (e.g. push, pull, hit, bump); words that describe movement (e.g. fast, slow, left, right, up, down); and words that describe position of objects (e.g. high, low, above, between, under). Create a word wall or Wordle chart, such as the one shown in Figure 7.3.

Figure 7.3 Wordle chart for movement words

Teaching point: As a follow-up to the creation of the word wall, to reinforce the meanings of the words, it may be useful to ask the children to mime or role-play to demonstrate combinations of these words (e.g. moving to the left slowly, rolling to the right, moving a pencil from below to above their desk). The action and position words encountered in this activity can be used in literacy activities, such as creating illustrated stories or making claymation video sequences to illustrate their meaning. Children's products can be collected and used in their assessment portfolio.

PHYSICAL SCIENCE 97

Moving through an obstacle course

SCIENCE INQUIRY SKILLS *Communicate understanding through actions*

In this activity, the teacher will need to set up a series of action stations throughout the obstacle course using objects such as traffic cones or markers. Each station requires the children to move an object (such as a soccer ball) using the instructions at the station. For example, they could be asked to bounce the ball over something; push the ball or pull the ball through an opening/around something/to the right or left; slide the ball slowly/quickly and so on.

An extension to this activity might involve the children creating a station for their classmates or a mini-version back in the classroom for a toy (such as a car).

> **Teaching point:** After completing the obstacle course activity, the children can be asked to reflect on what they did—perhaps through writing or drawing.

Extension ideas

Role-play

SCIENCE INQUIRY SKILLS *Explore and communicate through role-play*

This episode varies from the previous activity as it incorporates a role-play sequence that requires the children to think more deeply about what might cause something to move. The teacher guides this role-play sequence through the selection of scenarios—for example, the situation in which tugboats help to dock a large ship. A group of four or five children can link together to pretend to be the large ship, while other children can pretend to be the tugboats, pushing and pulling the ship to get it perfectly into the dock. Afterwards, discuss what was happening during the role-play. Repeat this kind of scenario with other sequences—for example, children pretend to be a horse pulling a carriage, a person pushing/pulling a lawn mower, stroller or shopping trolley. Ensure to draw out the push and pull aspects of the movement. Children can make suggestions for each scenario. Encourage them to give detail before the scenario is enacted—for example, what is the object, how does it move, what causes it to move?

> **Teaching point:** Through questioning, the teacher gains feedback about the extent of children's understanding of the activity. Again, children's notions may not be correct or complete at this stage, but the important thing is for them to consider the concept of movement. Teachers can provide input where they feel concepts or language can be developed appropriately.

Collecting and classifying forms of transport

SCIENCE INQUIRY SKILLS *Collect and sort data, classify*

Over a period of weeks, ask children to take photographs or collect images of as many different forms of transport as possible. Some examples are shown in Figure 7.4. Ask children to suggest ways of classifying and grouping the images—for example, modern transport or olden-day transport; human, animal or engine powered; two, four or many wheeled. Some modes of transport may not have wheels—for example, boats and sleds. Encourage children to classify the images in different ways. Perhaps use simple graphing to illustrate the frequency of different types of transport images collected.

Figure 7.4 Children may classify in different ways (a) a three-wheeled car and (b) segways

Classify

SCIENCE INQUIRY SKILLS *Use multiple ways to sort information*

Using images, real objects or word cards (or a combination), have children in groups or as a whole class take turns in classifying objects by movement characteristics. Use named hoops or string circles as areas for classifying in many different ways (or use a virtual version of the activity on the IWB). Sometimes there may be two classifications, sometimes more. If appropriate, the children could attempt classification of objects that could be placed in two or more categories, thus requiring an intersection. Examples for classification include:

- things that can move or can't move
- things that sometimes move, always move or never move

PHYSICAL SCIENCE   99

- things that are alive and move, and things that are not alive and move (living and non-living may need some prior work—this can be a difficult concept for some children)
- things that move by themselves and things that need help to move.

PHYSICAL SCIENCE 2 ————————————————————————————

Collisions

- **Science understanding:** When objects collide, they:
    - may or may not change shape
    - may change shape in different ways
    - may or may not return to their original shape, or
    - may have observable properties that cause them to behave differently. (This is a chemical science understanding.)

People use science when making objects for our benefit—for example, safer cars, bicycle helmets or elbow/knee guards for skating.

- **Nature of science:** Science involves exploring and observing the environment, and questioning and describing changes in objects and events.

OVERVIEW

This unit outlines some possible teaching and learning episodes around ideas about what happens when two objects collide. Depending on the characteristics of the objects (e.g. size, shape, mass, material) and the characteristics of the contact (e.g. speed, angle/direction, relative size of objects), the objects will behave in different ways (e.g. bend, smash, compress and return to original shape, do nothing). This unit provides great opportunities for children to complete play and guided play experiences, as well as conducting focused investigations to test ideas.

A collision is when two objects make contact with each other. The objects could both be moving or one may be stationary. The results of a collision may be a change to both objects, one object or neither object.

EPISODE 1 ··

Crashing to earth

Discussion stimulus

SCIENCE INQUIRY SKILLS *Observe, respond to questions, ask questions and hypothesise*

Use the stimulus picture in Figure 7.5 or a similar image to prompt a discussion about collisions. What does it mean for objects to collide? What objects could collide? Encourage children to think beyond vehicle collisions to examples such as hitting a ball with a bat, bouncing a ball, bumping into a post, falling over when playing or dropping a pencil on the floor.

Figure 7.5 Stimulus image: the boulder and car have behaved differently after the collision. Which object has changed shape? Which has stayed the same? Why did the objects behave differently? Think of other collisions in which one of the objects changes shape and the other remains the same

Teaching point: These questions prompt the children to think about the nature of collisions, and examples from their daily lives and experiences. This is also a great opportunity to create or add to a word wall to expand children's vocabulary—what are some words that we use to describe collisions (e.g. bump, crash, hit, slap, thump) and some words that describe the outcomes of collisions (e.g. crumple, snap, bounce, crush, break)?

PHYSICAL SCIENCE 101

Demonstration activity

SCIENCE INQUIRY SKILLS *Predict and experiment, organise information, compare observations and predictions*

SCIENTIFIC LITERACY *Representations (in this activity, tabular) have specific characteristics that allow them to show information in different ways*

On a demonstration table, have a variety of objects that can be dropped on to a surface to create a collision. Try to source a variety of objects that will behave in different ways, such as a tennis ball, ball of play dough, slime, fresh egg (if you're feeling brave), boiled egg, eraser, balloon, stone, plastic bottle, ice and sugar cube. Label these objects with numbers.

Also have a variety of surfaces on to which the objects could be dropped, such as a carpet square, foam sheet, cardboard, brick/tile/paver, thin sheet of play dough, tray of sand and sheet of bubble wrap. Label these surfaces with letters.

Use a plastic ground sheet under the demonstration area to limit mess. If possible, have a digital microscope or image projector/visualiser to allow all children to clearly see the results after the collision. Create a set of number cards and a set of letter cards that correspond to the objects and the surfaces. Taking turns, children select a number card and letter card to determine the collision they must conduct. When each child has their object and collision surface, ask the class to predict what the result will be and explain their reasoning. Tabulate objects, surface, predictions and results on the IWB. Ask each child to simply drop the object from shoulder height on to the selected surface. When possible, use digital technology to examine any changes in either the object or the surface, then project on to the IWB. Discuss how the results align with the predictions.

From children's predictions and the actual experimental outcomes, make a list of what they believe is the reason why various objects and surfaces behaved in the way they did.

> **Teaching point:** This is a great opportunity to expand children's scientific literacy skills by discussing the use of a table to organise data. Asking the children questions such as 'Why is the table helpful for organising our information?' 'What information does a table have?' and 'How do we make a table?' can elicit ideas about the essential features of a table (e.g. headings, columns, rows) and illustrate to the children how different representations can help us make comparisons, look for patterns, organise, analyse and communicate scientific data and ideas.

Children can draw a picture of themselves conducting the experiment. Ask them to label the object and surface, and give some words or phrases that describe what happened. At the conclusion of this activity, ask the children what else they would like to know about or investigate. Are there any other objects or surfaces they would like to try? Would they

102 TEACHING EARLY YEARS MATHEMATICS, SCIENCE AND ICT

like to conduct the experiment in other ways—for example, dropping from a greater height, throwing the object on to the surface?

> **Teaching point:** The teacher could ask the children to make predictions about what would happen if different objects or surfaces were used. This would allow the children to apply their knowledge to new scenarios and the teacher to assess their understanding of concepts and their ability to apply their knowledge. The children's responses and the products they create provide multiple opportunities for assessment.

EPISODE 2

Slow-motion wrecks

Activity

SCIENCE INQUIRY SKILLS *Explore and observe, record observations, collect data digitally (in this case through digital images)*

In pairs, children complete a four-photo (approximately) sequence of a slow motion collision between hand-held objects—for example, play dough models, plastic or foam cups, or balloons. Examples of different scenarios are shown in Figure 7.6. Photos can be taken by an adult or a competent child, and then downloaded on to a PowerPoint or similar. Children can annotate with or without the help of an adult. The photo sequence should be a) before contact, b) initial contact, c) further contact and, d) ceasing contact. The objects in collision may behave in different ways, which should be captured in the photo sequence. Some objects—for example, the play dough models—should squash out of shape and retain their new shape; the plastic or foam cup should collapse but may regain some of its initial shape; the balloons should change shape on collision but regain their shape unless they burst. Children can predict what they believe will happen to the two objects before the photo sequence, then try to explain the behaviour of the objects in their annotations.

PHYSICAL SCIENCE   103

Figure 7.6a   Play dough balls in a collision sequence. Both objects change shape and retain the new shape

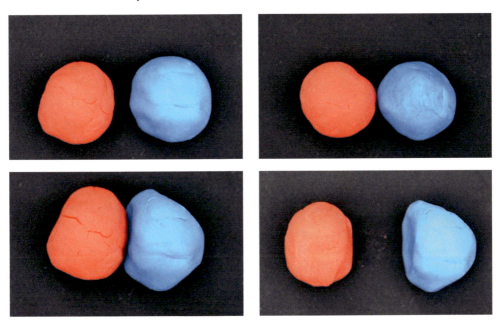

Figure 7.6b   Balloons during and after collision. Both objects change shape but revert to their original shape

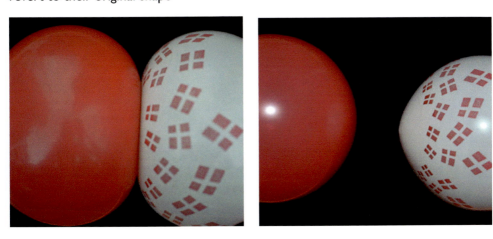

Figure 7.6c A rock and play dough ball before and after collision. The rock remains unchanged and the play dough changes shape on impact and retains its new shape

Figure 7.6d A rock and balloon during and after collision. The rock remains unchanged and the balloon changes shape on impact but returns to its original shape

Figure 7.6e Two rocks during and after collision. Both rocks retain their shape during and after collision. Perhaps a little scarring occurs

Viewing

SCIENCE INQUIRY SKILLS *Share and compare observations and ideas*

When the photo sequences have been downloaded, view the finished products as a class. Ask children to explain why they think the different objects behaved differently during and after collision.

Teaching point: This is another opportunity to expand children's scientific literacy skills by discussing the use of photographic images as a means to record and represent data and share observations. Children should suggest ideas such as 'It's easier to show a picture than to describe some things in words' or 'Things that happen quickly are difficult to see or to describe but a photo can show what happened'. The children's products can be added to their digital portfolio for use as assessment.

EPISODE 3

Scratch and dent hunt

Field trip

SCIENCE INQUIRY SKILLS *Observe using senses, collect data*

Considering safety, children move around the school grounds looking for evidence of collisions. Examples could include scratches and bumps on furniture or trees, dents on cars, scratches on paintwork, injuries to other children (grazes or scratches), footprints, ball games in progress, marks on a bat or racquet, broken, crushed or smashed containers. This activity could be done as a large group, with children discussing each piece of collision evidence as it is found. Alternatively, children could work in groups with adult supervision. Before leaving the classroom, revise with the children what a collision may entail, and what the signs of a collision might be. Use digital cameras or pencil and paper to record the collisions found.

Figure 7.7 When a foot collides with the ground, it may leave a footprint, depending on the surface: (a) a baboon's footprint, (b) a seagull's footprints

Discussion of observations

SCIENCE INQUIRY SKILLS *Share and discuss ideas and observations with others*

This part of the activity can be conducted either while outside or when back in the classroom—or both. When possible, ask about what may have caused the collisions and the resulting damage. Children may find examples and perhaps verbalise some of the following collision scenarios:

- Both objects are unscathed. (It is hard to find evidence of these, but they can be discussed—for example, walking on concrete may leave no evidence of the foot/concrete collision.)
- One object is unscathed and the other is damaged or changed.
- Both objects are damaged or changed.
- Both objects were moving when the collision occurred.
- One object was moving and one was stationary.

Teaching point: At the conclusion of this activity, the digital images gathered will provide an excellent opportunity to classify the collisions into the types listed above and perhaps combinations of them (e.g. both objects moving and only one changed, or one object moving and only one changed).

EPISODE 4

Softening the blow, protecting against injury during collisions

Brief discussion

SCIENCE INQUIRY SKILLS *Ask and respond to questions*
SCIENTIFIC LITERACY *Science knowledge can help us to make better decisions for the benefit of others and ourselves*

Gather a series of objects together for display that are examples of how we manufacture protective equipment to prevent damage to ourselves when we have a collision—for example, cushioned shoes to protect our feet from impact when walking or running, cushions to soften the impact when we sit, bicycle helmets, goalpost padding, protective wear for sports people. Also include video footage from the internet of slow-motion deployment of car airbags. Discuss with children how each of these things helps to lessen the impact on a person in times of collision and the importance of using equipment to keep us safe. Relate this to how science helps us decide how to make things safer for our use.

Construction

SCIENCE INQUIRY SKILLS *Make predictions, explore and answer questions, manipulate materials and test ideas*

The goal of this activity is for children, with or without adult assistance, to create or modify an object to make it safer in the event of a collision. The classic example for this is to use a raw egg and devise ways of protecting it from a short fall. Eggs can be messy, and the activity can be wasteful if many are used. This activity could be conducted as an initial teacher-led demonstration to reduce the mess and waste, and give a graphic understanding of the value of protection from a collision. Ways of protecting the egg could include wrapping it in foam, surrounding it in crushed paper and putting it inside a foam cup, or constructing a parachute from a plastic bag, string and elastic bands.

Let the children make some suggestions, and don't forget that great things can be learned from experiments that don't achieve their goal. Have the children make predictions before testing their ideas. This could be done through the use of a chart on which the children can use ticks or crosses to predict successes and failures. Discuss with children other means of protecting the egg and why some protections may have succeeded and others failed.

> **Teaching point:** This is an example of a topic that lends itself to a focus on concepts from both physical and chemical sciences. The success and failure of different materials could be linked to chemical science understandings such as: objects are made from materials with observable properties; or materials can be changed in various ways and for various purposes. Children could investigate the use of the same material in different ways (e.g. paper wrapped around the egg compared with paper scrunched up beneath the egg) or the use of two or more different materials in the same way (e.g. wrapping the egg in paper, plastic film, foam, etc.).

EXTENSION IDEAS
* The ideas on collisions in this topic could be linked to the creation of sound by various sources (another physical science understanding). This might include crashes and breakages; musical instruments such as pianos, drums and xylophones; household objects such as door-knockers.
* Extend the range of collisions to include one moving, one stationary; both moving towards each other head on; moving towards each other from different directions; and both moving in the same direction but at different speeds.
* Discuss with the children whether collisions only happen between solid objects—for example, what happens when you are in the ocean and a wave hits you? What does it feel like when you 'belly flop' into a swimming pool? Can you feel water from the shower or rain landing on you—why might that be?
* Compare the outcomes of collisions with regular balloons with the outcomes of the same collisions with water-filled balloons (water bombs)—what might be causing the differences?

Planning and reflection

Use the Planning and Reflection for Teaching template in Chapter 1 to more deeply consider and make personal decisions about the pedagogy, curriculum and assessment possibilities or requirements for this unit.

Making ICT integral to a science lesson sequence: Biology

In this chapter, we have deliberately placed a stronger emphasis on the integration of ICT into the teaching and learning of a biological science topic about offspring to highlight the powerful and exciting opportunities that ICT affords modern science classrooms. Where possible, we will indicate the ICT competencies of:

- investigating
- creating
- communicating
- managing and operating, and
- safe and ethical use.

Offspring

- **Science understanding:** Plants and animals have offspring, which grow to be similar to the parents. Offspring have needs and rely on parents to different extents.
- **Nature of science:** Exploring and observing examples and features of offspring present in the environment.

MAKING ICT INTEGRAL TO A SCIENCE LESSON SEQUENCE: BIOLOGY   111

OVERVIEW

Children in the first years of schooling generally have an interest in (and often a love of) young creatures, such as puppies, kittens or human babies. These children are often also intrigued by concepts such as: Who am I? Why am I me? Where did I come from? To capitalise on these inherent interests, this learning sequence outlines ways of engaging young learners in basic concepts of the life-cycle, with a specific focus on the offspring of living things—particularly animals, but also plants.

This sequence will be outlined with an emphasis on possible ways of foregrounding the incorporation of ICT to enhance the teaching and learning process.

EPISODE 1

Young plants and animals

SCIENCE INQUIRY SKILLS *Observe, listen and respond to questions*

View, listen, and discuss

As a focus to stimulate discussion, share/read books (fiction or non-fiction) about baby animals. These books can be found online and projected on the IWB. There are numerous stories about baby animals, such as *Make Way for Ducklings* and *The Ugly Duckling*. The teacher needs to decide whether the books to be shared are age and content appropriate.

Figure 8.1 *Make Way for Ducklings* statue in Boston, the setting of the story

112   TEACHING EARLY YEARS MATHEMATICS, SCIENCE AND ICT

ICT teaching point: Interactive books are becoming increasingly common in classrooms, which means that even young children can make brief comments and notes on the books. These books can be shared on the IWB as well as on devices such as tablets.

ICT COMPETENCE   *Investigate with teacher guidance, through a knowledge source*

Other factual books are available, with illustrations and text that are able to be projected and shared. Some books are narrated, while others are not; again, a decision needs to be made about which is more appropriate. Such books are excellent for developing science understanding and literacy skills. This is also an opportunity to introduce vocabulary such as young, offspring, baby or parent.

Complete a similar sequence but with a focus on plants, introducing words such as seed, seedling, sapling and tree.

ICT COMPETENCE   *Manage and operate digital information sources*
ICT COMPETENCE   *Safe and ethical use of the internet*

When using these online books on the IWB, share the process of accessing them with children. Through modelling, this will help the children understand the methods used to safely find desired materials online. As the children's skills develop, ask for their assistance in searching for materials, considering things such as keywords.

Broaden the discussion

SCIENCE INQUIRY SKILLS *Respond to questions and share knowledge*
SCIENTIFIC LITERACY   *Children develop new science vocabulary*
ICT COMPETENCE   *Create a teacher-generated product with children's assistance*

Ask children to name any species of animals they know. Ask whether they know the name of the creature's offspring—for example, lion and cub, cat and kitten, swan and cygnet. While doing this, the teacher can be using Wordle (online word chart creation software) to create a record of the discussion, which will serve as a base for additional learning as the learning sequence progresses. As a visual representation, Wordle adjusts the size of the printing based on the frequency of the included word—for example, in Figure 8.2, the word *cub* is used most often and is therefore in larger print.

ICT COMPETENCE   *Create a child-generated product*
ICT COMPETENCE   *Share products and communicate with other children*

Later, if children's reading and writing skills are sufficient, they can work in groups to create their own wordles about parents and offspring, replicating the technique modelled by the teacher. These wordles can be shared via the IWB, printed and displayed, or kept as part of the child's digital portfolio.

A similar activity can be undertaken with a focus on plants.

Figure 8.2 (a) Wordle can be used to determine and display children's current knowledge about parents and offspring; (b) a swan and cygnet

Matching Activity

SCIENCE INQUIRY SKILL   *Process and analyse information*
ICT COMPETENCE   *Create a teacher-generated product for consolidating children's learning*

From the information shared by children and that found through online books and sites, the teacher can make a matching activity to be used with the class via the IWB. Prepare a series of pictures and names of animals and their offspring that children must appropriately match by dragging and dropping. An example of a teacher-generated activity is shown in Figure 8.3.

ICT COMPETENCE   *Create a child-generated product*

If children are experienced enough and have the relevant skills (or if they can be taught the skills) they can make their own matching activities to share with their classmates. This can be done in a variety of ways, using both software and internet-based products.

Figure 8.3 Example of parent/offspring and name-matching activity

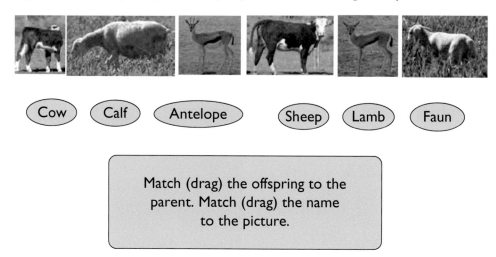

EPISODE 2

Case study of self

Representing information

SCIENCE INQUIRY SKILLS   *Communicate orally, listen, respond to questions, analyse data and information*
SCIENTIFIC LITERACY   *Data can be represented physically and representations can be transformed into different modes (e.g. from physical to digital to text)*

In a discussion circle, ask children to tell the class some facts about themselves or their families, such as number, age and sex of siblings. Choose some facts to gather data—for example, number of siblings. Place some marker cones in a line on the floor approximately 1 metre apart. Number the cones from 0 to 4 (or greater if some children have more siblings than this). Ask children (one at a time) to sit behind the cone that represents the number of siblings they have. A column graph with children's bodies will naturally develop. See Figure 8.4 for a diagram.

ICT COMPETENCE   *Manage data and store for later sharing*
ICT COMPETENCE   *Create a teacher and/or child-generated digital product*

Questions about the sibling graph can then be asked, such as: How many children in each column? Which column has the most children, and which has the least? Which is the most common number of siblings? Use a digital camera to capture each graph for later sharing

Figure 8.4 Representing data

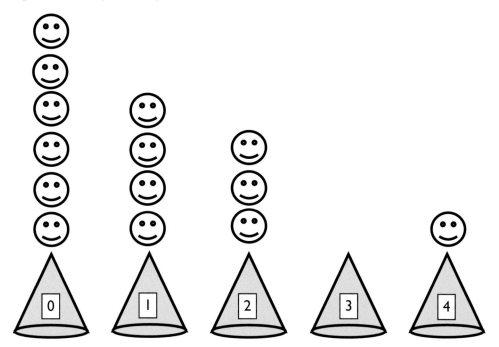

and display. The teacher and/or children can photograph the graphs. This is an opportunity to teach children how to use the digital camera, as well as skills for downloading, saving and naming images.

Further graphs can be made by focusing on different ideas such as children's hair or eye colour. The children may like to suggest characteristics to investigate. While we emphasise that data should, wherever possible, be collected with an authentic purpose, children enjoy activities such as these because they are learning about themselves and their classmates. There are many data collection and graphing packages available online. Select one or more to re-represent the data the class has gathered, to be shared on the IWB.

Bring the discussion back to the focus that everyone is the offspring of parents and that when they are older, the children may have offspring of their own.

Photo gallery

SCIENCE INQUIRY SKILLS *Plan, manipulate materials and compare*
ICT COMPETENCE   *Create teacher-generated resources for classroom use*

116 TEACHING EARLY YEARS MATHEMATICS, SCIENCE AND ICT

If possible, ask children to bring or email photos (digital copies, not family treasures) of themselves when they were babies. Take digital photos of the children as they are now. Place the photos side by side in PowerPoint format, ready to share with the class. As the images are shared with the class, ask children to make some comments about themselves, such as how they have or have not changed. What do they like now that they didn't like when they were babies? Try to elicit ideas of growth and change, but also how some things perhaps do not change. Ask children to think of three factual sentences to share with the class about themselves, highlighting the similarities or differences between now and when they were babies.

> **ICT teaching point:** Digital cameras have revolutionised means of recording and sharing learning experiences. This importance was highlighted by Prain (2006, p. 180), who noted 'the growing recognition of the insufficiency of written language on its own to represent processes of reasoning, measuring, and explanations in science activity'.

Digital photos can be taken and edited by children (with or without assistance) and used in many ways, including:

- to capture and chronicle major events of the school year
- to show a developmental sequence, such as when learning a new skill
- to promote problem-solving
- for science learning sequences, such as through time lapse
- to use in a digital storytelling sequence, such as claymation or slowmation stories
- to illustrate writing or a report
- to record work samples for sharing and portfolios.

ICT COMPETENCE   *Safe and ethical use of digital equipment and images*

Technical skills can be extended to image manipulation. Ethics of digital image use can be discussed in simple terms with children—for example, asking permission to take a classmate's photo, seeking approval to use the photo in an ICT product. Asking the children how they would feel if their photos were taken or used without permission will help develop an understanding of these safety and ethical issues.

ICT COMPETENCE   *Create teacher- and child-generated products*
ICT COMPETENCE   *Communicate using technology*
ICT COMPETENCE   *Manage data and files*

Set up a digital video camera on a tripod and record each child's presentation. Perhaps use a teacher assistant or parent to do this. Download and file these for sharing with the class and adding to the children's digital portfolio.

> **ICT teaching point:** Watching videos as a knowledge resource is a great means to engage children. Videos on a vast array of topics, specifically designed for young learners, are available from many sources. Always view the videos first to check for relevance to topic and age.

Video production and use of images have the power to capture much of the visual and spatial thinking that is vital for learning science (Ramadas 2009). Video technology is now available through most digital cameras and editing software is available as standard on most computer operating systems. Young children may make videos with varying levels of assistance. When children make videos, they:

- learn about the technology
- engage enthusiastically in the topic of the video
- revisit their new learning through the rehearsal phase, videoing phase, editing phase and sharing phase (a very powerful iterative learning process)
- can revisit the topic over time
- learn skills of focusing on key points (an important literacy skill), and
- can create and learn through visual, oral, auditory and kinaesthetic means.

Concept mapping

SCIENCE INQUIRY SKILLS *Plan and represent ideas*
ICT COMPETENCE *Create a visual representation of ideas*

Use questioning to elicit children's ideas about the needs of a human baby. With concept-mapping software (usually licensed to schools), create a visual representation of children's ideas. Figure 8.5 shows a sample concept map.

> **ICT teaching point:** Concept mapping allows children to visualise their ideas using one of the numerous websites or software programs designed for this purpose (check online for options). Concept maps are excellent to use at the beginning of a unit or topic to ascertain prior knowledge on the topic. More detail can then be added to them as learning progresses or at the end of the topic to show the change or development in knowledge. Images are supplied so that young children can easily use these programs before they are able to read or write. Additional images pertinent to the topic can be uploaded to make learning more focused or topic specific.

Figure 8.5 Concept map of baby's needs created by teacher and children using Kidspiration software

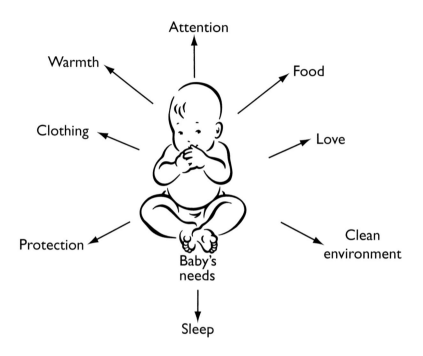

Concept mapping apps are now available for use with a broader range of devices. In addition to promoting children's ICT skills through the use of the software, concept mapping with young children allows them to learn to:

- organise thoughts and plan
- represent ideas in a non-linear way
- make connections between/among ideas
- apply new vocabulary and concepts and
- manipulate and change ideas as they develop.

As the creation of concept maps can be an iterative process—for example, before, during, and after a unit of work—they make excellent assessment tools for tracking children's development of understanding.

EPISODE 3 ⋯⋯⋯⋯⋯⋯⋯⋯⋯⋯⋯⋯⋯⋯⋯⋯⋯⋯⋯⋯⋯⋯⋯⋯⋯⋯⋯⋯⋯

Case studies—watching offspring grow

Observation activity

SCIENCE INQUIRY SKILLS	*Collect and record observations, discuss observations*
ICT COMPETENCE	*Investigate and collect data*
ICT COMPETENCE	*Create a teacher-generated product to guide children's investigating; create child-generated data and product*

With input from children's current knowledge, select some living things to watch as they grow and change. These could be silkworms in a box, bean seeds in pots or eggs of an aquatic creature in an aquarium. With or without adult help, children can work through a teacher-generated investigation guide to trace the development of the selected living things. This guide can be made using any of the numerous multimedia techniques such as VoiceThread or Wikis. The children can collect data using digital cameras, and create and annotate a time sequence using the photos.

> **ICT teaching point:** VoiceThread is a tool for creating digital conversations in the class. Check the VoiceThread website for possibilities. They can be made in several ways. Initially, it is best for the teacher to insert the image or photo and for the children to comment on that image/photo. When children have gained experience and confidence, they can take on the production role and create their own VoiceThread conversations. Children can use drawing tools, or they can use their voice or video, thus catering to different learning stages and needs. With young children, VoiceThread can be used with images alone, thus reducing the emphasis on written text.

In this offspring activity, the teacher could create a VoiceThread conversation of a life-cycle with images collected at the various stages. The children could then name each stage and add further information, thus creating a group VoiceThread product with shared knowledge. The act of integrating multiple modes of learning also potentially enhances children's understanding of a topic. VoiceThread conversations can be created by the whole class or by small groups, and even independently.

Wikis are helpful in direct teaching and scaffolding of young children's learning. They can be created as a class or in groups, and promote collaborative learning. In brief, a wiki is a website that is generally located in an online community such as Wikispaces. The use of wikis by teachers in the classroom encourages collaboration as well as communication of ideas, with children being able to contribute to and modify content (Roblyer & Doering 2013).

Both VoiceThreads and wikis can be useful assessment tools for the teacher.

120 TEACHING EARLY YEARS MATHEMATICS, SCIENCE AND ICT

EXTENSION IDEAS
Why do animals and plants have offspring? Big-picture discussion

SCIENCE INQUIRY SKILLS *Respond to questions, make predictions, share, discuss and compare ideas*
ICT COMPETENCE *Create a class-generated product*

Having investigated the concept of offspring for a period of time, it would be interesting to determine children's notions of the big-picture ideas of why living things have offspring. The discussion does not have to be complex or lengthy. Children's ideas can be recorded on a concept map.

> **Teaching point:** It is always interesting as a teacher to find out what conceptual understandings children have. Engaging in discussions will often reveal surprising insights. Even if the intended focus of the discussion proves to be beyond the reach of the children, it has still been a worthwhile activity for the teacher's understanding of the class.

The discussion can lead to children considering their own future and past. They may discuss their parents, grandparents or other ancestors, as well as their thoughts about the possibility that one day they may have offspring of their own. There are many books, videos and other online learning resources that address these topics. Concept-mapping software can be used to create simple family trees. Again, depending on the age and skills of the children, this might be a teacher demonstration, teacher-guided lesson, or children working independently or in groups.

How are offspring similar or different to parents?

ICT COMPETENCE *Investigate using online tools*
ICT COMPETENCE *Investigate and collect digital data*

- Use YouTube clips or web cams to explore different species' similarities and differences.
- Conduct a field trip in the school grounds, a nearby park or another environment to detect and record (using cameras) offspring, including those of plants and insects.
- Create and observe classroom or school-constructed habitats such as aquaria, terraria, flower and vegetable gardens or chicken pens. Capture data and images.

What do young plants and animals need to grow?

ICT COMPETENCE *Investigate using the internet*
ICT COMPETENCE *Safe use of the internet*

- Find out what children know about the needs of offspring, plants, mammals, fish, birds or insects. Investigate further by modelling safe internet usage.
- Using ICT, discuss and investigate offspring's need for food, protection, shelter, guidance—talk about dependence and independence, number of offspring, readiness for independence. Figure 8.6 illustrates possible representation of the identified needs.

Figure 8.6 Collection of images to illustrate different offspring needs

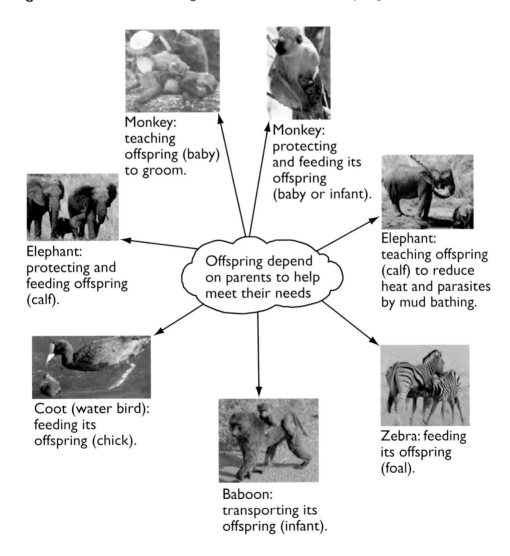

122 TEACHING EARLY YEARS MATHEMATICS, SCIENCE AND ICT

ICT teaching point: In the early years of schooling, children need guidance when using the internet and other digital tools. The teacher must determine the level of support needed, and will often model the usage on the IWB to help scaffold safe and appropriate use of the internet. The power of the internet lies in its real-time ability to assist children with research topics of interest. Guided internet experiences can be provided for children in the form of WebQuests and DiscoveryMissions. All ICT learning experiences provide opportunities to develop and strengthen children's cross-curricular skills. Using the internet and creating products can provide excellent opportunities for developing critical literacy and multiliteracies, as well as allowing teachers to assess children's progress in the development of conceptual understanding and their ICT competencies.

Planning and reflection

Use the Planning and Reflection for Teaching template in Chapter 1 to more deeply consider and make personal decisions about the pedagogy, curriculum and assessment possibilities or requirements for this unit.

Mathematics in the first three years of schooling

Overview

The early years mathematics curriculum lays the foundation for continued and further study of mathematics in the later years. Before children commence school, they possess considerable intuitive mathematics knowledge, derived from experiencing and interacting with their environment. In the early years of schooling, the teacher's role is to capitalise and build on children's mathematical knowledge, to shape and develop children's mathematical knowledge and skills.

Chapters 9 to 12 focus on the teaching and learning of mathematics. This chapter begins with a snapshot of the mathematics knowledge that young children bring to school. It also presents research on the teaching styles of effective early mathematics teachers. This is followed by a consideration of play-based learning environments, questioning approaches to extend children's mathematical thinking and reasoning, contexts and classrooms routines for teaching and learning mathematics and assessment of mathematics learning. The chapters that follow address three broad strands of mathematics curriculum in the first three years of schooling. In these years, a strong curricular emphasis is placed on the development of children's understanding of number and their number sense, along with ideas for developing patterning (the foundation of algebraic thinking). This topic is covered in Chapter 10. Given less curricular emphasis, but of equal importance to children's mathematical education, are statistics and probability (discussed in Chapter 11) and geometry and measurement (discussed in Chapter 12). Although these curriculum areas are presented separately, it is often the case that activities will lend themselves to developing concepts across these areas. For example, activities involving measurement may provide opportunities to collect and present data as well as develop number sense. Classroom examples presented in this chapter often reflect this interconnectedness. Opportunities for developing a range of mathematical skills also exist in curriculum areas beyond mathematics. Examples of these can be seen in the preceding chapters on science.

Young children's mathematical knowledge

Young children have sophisticated intuitive knowledge of mathematical concepts before they come to school (e.g. Ben-Zeev & Star 2008; Carpenter & Lehrer 1999; Copley 2006; Thompson et al. 2005). Take the concept of division, for example. Young children have a highly developed sense of sharing, and hence the concept of division, well before they have ever been taught about the mathematical operation of division. This is clearly evident when they are observed diligently distributing fair shares with their friends. Their well-developed sense of 'fair' ensures that everything is shared equally. Even if at times the share favours themselves, they can justify it, and are happy to state that it is 'fair'. The mathematical knowledge children bring to school is intuitive, and highly meaningful and sensible to them.

A study into the provision of early mathematics in learning centres in the year before school and during the first year of school was reported by Thompson and colleagues (2005). It examined children's achievement on items classified as number, space and measurement tasks. The results of this assessment indicated that children are quite familiar with terms such as smaller, more, longest and shortest; and ordinal positions such as second place. Children could identify properties of shapes, with nearly half of the children able to identify a cone and a cylinder, curved sides of shapes, and that a cube has square faces. As stated in the report, 'The children in this study continually surprised teachers and researchers by the numeracy they knew and could do.' (2005, p. xvi). The most difficult items were those requiring mental subtraction of change from $1.00, sequencing of teen numbers, matching a picture to a number sentence and reading clock times of half past the hour. Different patterns of achievement were evident—for example, in general, girls performed better than boys.

Other research within the study by Thompson et al. (2005) identified a variety of classroom organisational arrangements and mathematical teaching styles. They also found that teachers' beliefs about mathematics and children's learning of mathematics influenced effectiveness. They classified teachers as being one of three types—*connectionist*, *transmission* and *discovery* teachers—according to how they taught their mathematics lessons. As the term suggests, transmission teachers viewed mathematics as 'discrete skills, conventions, and procedures to be taught and practised' (2005, p. 9). Although discovery teachers provided rich learning environments with the aim of children discovering mathematics knowledge, learning opportunities were not capitalised upon and mathematical knowledge connections were not made by the children. The connectionist teachers were found to be the most effective. They made strong efforts to assist children to build connections between the activity, the mathematics knowledge of focus and the children's own knowledge, through the use of appropriate language. In summary, effective mathematical teaching practices were found to be those with a clear emphasis on concepts and thinking, where children were encouraged to share their strategies for and solutions to particular tasks, and where children's strategies were valued.

Play-based learning environments for mathematics learning

Play-based approaches are centred on rich learning environments that invite and beckon children to spontaneously engage and hence develop important problem-solving strategies, reasoning skills and social processes in group situations. Play-based learning may be considered to involve contexts in which children develop an understanding of their world by actively engaging with people, objects and representations (Department of Education, Employment and Workplace Relations [DEEWR] 2009). While play-based approaches are often hallmarks of quality pre-school learning environments, they are also important in learning mathematics in the first three years of school. Some rich environments are more disposed to building young children's mathematical processes than others. For example, having a variety of vessels (cups, buckets, spoons, scoops, mugs, jars) in the sandpit may result in children naturally measuring, counting how many of these vessels are required to fill that vessel, determining which vessel has the greatest capacity, ordering the vessels according to how much they can hold, and even performing simple proportional calculations, such as three cups to fill one bucket means nine cups to fill three buckets. Astute teachers will note the play in which the children are engaging, and encourage mathematical thinking through the questions they ask—for example:

- Which vessel holds the most sand? How do you know?
- How many cups of sand can the truck carry?
- How many truckloads need to be removed to make a pond for our goldfish?
- Are there two containers here that hold exactly the same amount of sand?
- Could there be two containers that look different from each other that can hold the same amount of sand? Is this possible? Why/why not?
- Are there any containers that hold exactly half the amount of sand as another container? How will you know?

Play-based environments are characterised by the provision of a range of resources, with the teacher observing and noticing children as they interact with those resources. Learning is extended as the teacher sits beside children and asks them about their activity, then prompts their thinking. The following is a vignette of a teacher extending a child's mathematical thinking (DEEWR 2010).

> *Classroom example*: A child is playing with lengths of wood. The teacher sits beside the child and asks whether any length of wood is as tall as the teacher. This requires the child to use direct comparison of the lengths of wood with the teacher's height. The teacher asks the child whether he could find one piece of wood that would be the same height as him. Upon further discussion, the child informs the teacher that he wants to make this piece of wood into a stop sign, and the teacher discusses the shape of stop signs. This draws the child's thinking to shapes of common objects in the environment and also reinforces the language and properties of two-dimensional shapes.

This activity could be extended from this point to engage other children in the discussion about stop signs and their shapes. Further activities could include an environment walk where children notice the shapes of signs in their neighbourhood. The children could take photos of these various signs, print them and display them on the wall, grouping them according to their shape. The signs also provide important literacy opportunities as children start to associate particular words or icons with their meaning and consider the ways in which they communicate instructions to citizens. Sometimes, for safety reasons, signs have rounded corners and teachers will need to point out to children that many shapes such as squares, triangles and rectangles are not rounded at the points where their sides meet (see Figure 9.1).

Figure 9.1   Circular, square, triangular and rectangular neighbourhood signs

Wherever appropriate, it is important to utilise play-based learning so that mathematical thinking is developed in a meaningful context. This ensures that mathematical skills are not taught in isolation. Examples of contexts for early years classrooms include:

- the supermarket
- the farmers' market
- the shoe shop
- the school canteen
- the dress-up shop
- the jungle
- the forest
- the ocean.

Not only do such contexts provide a rich background for mathematical learning, but they encourage learning in other curriculum areas as well. The physical act of creating the context engages children's imaginations and their capacity for make-believe and role-play. Building the context can take place over several days or weeks. The context provides a meaningful anchor point from which the teacher can use imagination to create targeted learning experiences. Van Oers (2010), for example, described how a classroom shoe shop became a focus of rich mathematical investigations for young children.

Taking the theme of a shoe shop further, other ideas for mathematics learning can be imagined. The children can classify the shoes in order to be able to display the shoes in the shop. With or without adult help, the children can make cardboard boxes for the shoes, which will entail cutting and constructing three-dimensional nets of rectangular prisms. As an extension, older children can price the shoes according to their own invented criteria. The pricing of the shoes could be a group project, with children allocated to a particular category of shoe that they price and then justify the price to the rest of the class. When the shop is complete, the children can take turns in being the shopkeeper who must count back change for the customers who come in to buy the shoes.

> **Teaching point:** The teacher needs to decide whether children are ready to create nets of 3D objects and the level of assistance required. The teacher also needs to consider the readiness of children to engage in activities involving counting of money and counting back of change. In the earliest school years, children start by counting and ordering small collections of coins. Simple pricing done by the teacher may be needed in such instances.

When choosing topics, it is important to consider children's background, thus linking school and family life; however, this is not to say that other themes cannot be brought into the classroom to provide contexts for learning experiences.

Children have never experienced life with dinosaurs, but they are very interested in these prehistoric creatures. With technology and other resources, the teacher can extend children's knowledge of new and unfamiliar contexts, but can embed the learning experiences in familiar routines. A collection of dinosaurs can be sorted and counted according to various classifications: meat eaters, plant eaters; tree dwellers, ground dwellers, water dwellers; movement characteristics and so on (see Figure 9.2).

Figure 9.2 Ground dwelling dinosaur collection

Questioning to extend children's mathematical vocabulary, thinking and reasoning

In situations that are new and interesting, children typically verbalise their thinking or ask questions. For example, the teacher might come to class wearing a large, floppy hat that is uncharacteristic. This causes children to verbalise such questions as: Why are you wearing that hat? Where did you get that? Are you going somewhere special? They may also notice things about the hat: that hat is really big, that hat has lots of flowers on it and they are all pink, that hat has a ribbon. Teachers can capitalise on this natural tendency to talk through questioning to promote mathematical thinking and learning.

Thwaite and McKay (2013) outlined key features of classroom discourse to promote young children's learning. Observing effective early years teachers, they noted how the teacher's questioning controlled the structure of the discourse as children naturally initiated it, channelled the conversation and encouraged turn-taking to engage all children. In particular, asking 'how' and 'why' questions

130   TEACHING EARLY YEARS MATHEMATICS, SCIENCE AND ICT

encouraged children to extend their thinking. Specialist vocabulary was introduced by helping children make meaningful connections between informal language and the specific language of the topic. The following classroom example shows how a set of play equipment becomes a valuable learning experience in developing understanding of three-dimensional shapes and their properties.

Classroom example: The teacher shows children a collection that includes:

- round balls of various sizes (exercise ball, tennis ball, table tennis ball, golf ball, marble, soccer ball)
- a football (e.g. Rugby ball—that is, not a soccer ball)
- plastic ice-hockey puck.

The teacher guides the children in an exploration of their properties—for example, by rolling, bouncing, bouncing on (the exercise ball), throwing or catching as appropriate. The children notice that the Rugby ball (ovoid shape) does not behave (bounce or roll) in the same way as the round balls. They explore the stitching on the ball and count the number of sections. They then count the number of sections on the soccer ball and the tennis ball. The children describe the round balls as 'round', and the teacher asks whether all the items in the collection are round. The children discuss the differences in the surfaces of the round balls and the teacher asks whether the Rugby ball is round. The teacher then states that the shape of the round balls is called a sphere. The children can help develop a shared definition of a sphere, and subsequent regular usage of the word will help to embed its meaning.

The teacher asks whether there are any other spheres in the collection. The children explore the hockey puck and the teacher asks whether the hockey puck is like the spheres. The children identify the circle on the top and bottom of the hockey puck. After realising that the hockey puck doesn't roll easily end over end, the children then put the puck on its side and roll it. They exclaim that it is like a wheel, but it doesn't have a hole through the middle like a wheel. The teacher rubs the top (flat) surface of the hockey puck, stating that this is a round shape, but that it is different to the round ball, because the ball is a sphere. The teacher labels the two circles of the hockey puck as faces and describes them as the flat surfaces of the hockey puck, but mentions that other shapes also have faces. The teacher asks: Does the Rugby ball have flat faces? Do the spheres have flat faces?

The teacher encourages children to look around the room at other objects to see whether faces can be identified. The teacher also asks whether there are other spheres that children have seen in their own neighbourhoods. In this short investigation, children have sorted and classified a collection of objects and learnt new vocabulary associated with 3D shapes: sphere, faces. The next day's lesson builds on these new words and more 3D shapes are included in the collection. Informal language of 'round' and 'flat circles' has been replaced with sphere and faces.

In rich learning environments such as this, children learn new language of mathematics through skilful teacher questioning and problem-posing. Other examples of this approach to developing mathematics concepts appear throughout Chapters 10 to 13.

Context-based mathematics learning

Creating contexts or utilising existing contexts within the school can provide rich and authentic mathematical learning opportunities. For example, many schools have undertaken sustainability projects that include the establishment of a kitchen garden. The garden provides numerous opportunities for mathematics learning, both in play-based and more directed learning environments. Some ideas for developing mathematical thinking in the kitchen garden with young children are presented below. They draw and extend on the ideas in a case study from *Educators Belonging, Being and Becoming: Educators' Guide to the Early Learning Framework for Australia* (DEEWR 2010). In the following chapters, we make explicit links to different mathematical strands of number and algebra, statistics and probability, and geometry and measurement to demonstrate the opportunities to focus on concepts across mathematics. Note also the many opportunities for making links to other curriculum areas.

EPISODE 1 ···

Who lives in the garden?

Observation task

Children observe and note the creatures that live in the garden. They draw pictures or take digital photos of animals such as slugs, snails, worms, slaters, cockroaches, caterpillars, butterflies, lizards and birds. Some creatures may not be seen directly, but evidence of their existence is apparent, such as eaten leaves, droppings or diggings. The children sort these creatures according to number of legs. The children can make graphical representations of the number of creatures seen over the course of a term.

> **Teaching point:** This activity develops number and algebra skills such as counting, the language of counting, connecting names with quantities, comparison and ordering, and statistics and probability skills such as collection and representation of data.

132   TEACHING EARLY YEARS MATHEMATICS, SCIENCE AND ICT

Mathematical problem-solving task

If there were 24 legs, what sorts of creatures could there be in the garden? This open-ended task (taken from Board of Studies 1997) has many possible solutions. In their collection, children might suggest that there are three spiders (eight legs) or four beetles (six legs). They might also suggest a collection of animals with legs that total 24—for example, two spiders, one ant and a sparrow. These collections could be represented on the IWB, with the whole class counting and sharing solutions.

> **Teaching point:** This activity is an opportunity for children to engage in problem-solving, to develop number facts (opportunities for repeated addition, grouping and arrays) and for the teacher to emphasise that real-world problems often have more than one solution.

Children might suggest that there are 24 snails, as snails only have one leg (strictly known as a foot). Snails technically do not have limbs, and their 'foot' is actually a muscle, but it is helpful to have something in the collection that gives a value of 1. This would be a useful time to discuss this feature of snails, and to make links to science and the characteristics of living things.

EPISODE 2 ···

Growing plants

Planting the garden

New plants are to be planted in the garden. Each plant requires different planting distances. For example:

- Snow peas: 5–10 centimetres apart
- Beetroot: 15 centimetres apart
- Tomatoes: 70 centimetres apart.

If the children have not yet engaged with formal units of measurement, before planting, with the teacher's guidance, the children can develop 'benchmarks' of these distances, such as a child's outspread hand, which may be approximately 10 centimetres and can be used to estimate 15 centimetres. Children can find pieces of wood, or even make up their own measuring devices from cardboard to help them determine how far apart the plants need to be planted.

> **Teaching point:** This activity provides further opportunities for children to work with number, and to engage in and describe planting patterns. They can also engage in

MATHEMATICS IN THE FIRST THREE YEARS OF SCHOOLING 133

> measurement to establish or reinforce the idea of benchmarking. It provides children with an experience of lengths and areas within the garden. The teacher could lead a discussion about different shapes in the garden.

For older children, a golden opportunity for promoting proportional reasoning is offered in planning the garden, which can also be modelled in the classroom. If there are two rows of cabbages with three cabbages in each row, how many cabbages will there be if we double both sides of the garden? Most children will readily state that there will be twelve cabbages, but through acting out this scenario, they will see that if they double both the length and the width of the garden, they will quadruple the area, and hence quadruple the number of cabbages. This can be readily acted out with six children (2×3) sitting on the floor pretending to be cabbages. Double one side (four cabbages) and then double the other side (six cabbages). There are now 24 cabbages in this garden. A further representation can be illustrated in terms of the side length of the garden. Place two rulers on the floor to show one length, then three rulers to show the other length. Then double the length of each side (four rulers and six rulers respectively). Very quickly, children can see how the area of the garden has increased by a lot more than double.

Monitoring plant growth

Children keep records of the growth of the plants. They determine the period of the germination of the seeds from the seed packet, then use the calendar to mark off the days until the seeds are expected to pop through the soil. Daily measurements of growth are recorded. Children take photos of the daily changes they see in the plants, noting new growth. They also use the information on the packet to determine expected harvest time, which is marked on the calendar. Digital images can be collected over time and collated to develop a growth sequence similar to a time lapse.

> **Teaching point:** This ongoing activity provides multiple opportunities to focus on aspects of measurement (e.g. time, height) and on statistics and probability (e.g. data collection, collation, representation). It is important, when introducing children to measurement of such attributes as height or depth, to reinforce the idea that these are all measurement of a linear attribute, collectively known as length.

Watering the plants

Watering the plants is done via the watering can. The amount of water provided to the plants is recorded and a roster for watering determined. The number and size of the holes in the watering can could serve as a point of discussion and opportunity for informal inverse

134 TEACHING EARLY YEARS MATHEMATICS, SCIENCE AND ICT

proportional reasoning. If there are fewer holes, will the water drain from the can more quickly or slowly? Which is the best-sized watering can for the seeds or seedlings? What about when the plants get bigger and stronger?

> **Teaching point:** The activities associated with watering the plants provide opportunities for creating a timetable (a roster), creating tables about water use (data collation) and for developing number concepts (inverse proportion).

EPISODE 3

The worm farm

As part of many kitchen garden projects, schools or classes maintain worm farms to provide fertiliser for the garden through the worms' castings. This also provides an opportunity for the recycling of organic material, such as fruit and vegetable scraps.

How many worms?

The worms in the worm farm are usually provided with its purchase. This is typically in the order of 1000 worms. This is a big number, and it would be impractical to count the worms. However, the experience of looking at 1000 worms is valuable to build conceptualisation of the magnitude of this number. For older children, numbers to 1000 are part of their curriculum and for children before this age, the number 1000 is potentially accessible to them, so the worm farm provides a good reference point for considering numbers in this range. The number of worms will increase as they begin to multiply. This means that the worm farm might need to expand into another worm farm container.

Feeding the worms

Careful records are kept in relation to the food provided to the worms. This is in the form of an organised list that is added to progressively. At the end of the week, the children can tally the amount of food of each type that has been consumed. Younger children can simply count the number of containers of food that were used. Older children could perhaps have some experience of weighing the food. The children can also investigate which particular foods the worms mostly favour. Data tables and simple graphical representations can be created.

Worm investigations

The worms can provide the context for simple addition, subtraction, multiplication and division problems. For example, there were three worms and four more came to join the worm farm because of the delicious food that was being served. An even more exciting investigation can occur when children are asked to imagine that there are only two worms in the worm farm but their number doubles each day. How many worms would there be at the end of the week? The word problems can be made simpler or harder, based on the numbers with which children are familiar.

Worm products

The amount of liquid produced by the worms can be monitored. The younger children can count the number of containers produced. For older children, this is a great way to consider capacity (how much a vessel can hold). The capacity of different vessels can be determined and the appropriate vessel decided upon to catch the liquid. This can be measured and also form the basis of problem-solving tasks based on capacity. For example, if it takes four cups of worm liquid to spread over our small garden, how many cups of worm liquid would be required if our garden's dimensions were doubled? How long does it take for the worms to produce one cup of liquid?

> **Teaching point:** The worm activities provide many opportunities to develop concepts associated with number (counting, basic number facts, place value), data (tables, graphs) and measurement (time, capacity, mass). As with all activities, it is up to the teacher to make decisions regarding the level of complexity that is expected of the children. There are many more questions and activities that could be completed, limited only by teachers' and children's imaginations. While many questions tend to focus on a yes/no or factual response, the questions should be framed in such a way that the children are required to use and explain their reasoning.

Classroom routines and mathematics learning

Daily routines established in the classroom can become rich and ongoing mathematics learning opportunities—for example:

- Marking the roll is a routine that occurs at least daily, which provides the opportunity for developing basic number and counting (as well as counting on and counting back). For example, how many children are away? How many are at school? How many boys and girls are present or away?
- The school timetable is a routine that follows the same pattern on most days. There are events that occur on a weekly basis, such as specialist music, sport or language lessons. This routine exposes children to longer periods of time—for example, the length of a week, a half-hour lesson or a one-hour timeslot. It allows the teacher to draw attention to days of the week or dates.

In many of the other activities outlined in this chapter, there are daily or weekly components. For example monitoring plant growth, watering plants, feeding the worm farm and measuring its output are all repeated activities. There are also examples in Chapters 6 and 12 where the children collect daily and weekly weather observations. Classroom routines give multiple opportunities for children to experience the order and duration of events and the time intervals between them.

Assessing mathematics learning

Classroom-based assessment

The items on many early assessments of mathematics often appear to focus on one specific skill or fact (e.g. count forwards, count backwards, find all the triangles, etc.), and this can lead to consideration of mathematics as a set of skills and procedures to be practised and memorised. The danger with mathematics assessments of this kind is that they overlook the thinking and problem-solving strategies that children bring to the mathematics task. Mathematics assessments of this type can also direct the teacher to explicit teaching of skills in isolation, possibly stemming from a belief that mathematics knowledge is hierarchical and that 'basic' skills must be learnt before new skills and knowledge can be taught. Mathematics assessments may, in fact, perpetuate the belief that mathematics should be taught in a transmission style to ensure that children can respond appropriately to items on the assessment.

To guide teaching and ensure successful learning of mathematics, assessment must be considered in relation to the importance of rich learning experiences and teaching contexts, as has been highlighted in this chapter. Assessment items should also reflect the learning activities in which children have engaged. For example, if children have used concrete materials in class to learn about particular concepts, assessment items should also allow them to show their understanding using similar materials. There are many ways in which learning can be assessed without requiring extensive written responses. Children can be asked to represent something in multiple ways—for example, by making drawings, arranging or manipulating physical objects or using symbols. Assessment of sequencing concepts can be done using physical materials or through storyboarding. Children can use number lines, blocks and counters to represent numerical relationships. They can create digital products that demonstrate their understanding—for example, a series of digital photos with annotations. Drawing pictures can be used to demonstrate ideas of direction or location.

As in all subjects, there are many ways in which evidence of children's learning can be collected and recorded. The list of examples above is not exhaustive. Such assessment items can be part of the children's ongoing learning or they can be specific assessment tasks. The teacher can record annotations on an ongoing basis for each child to build a profile of what the child can do. They can collect the children's work in digital or physical portfolios. There may be opportunities to interview children about their work or to video-record their manipulation and explanation of particular problem-solving tasks. Many examples of assessment methods were provided in Chapter 1—for example, observations, annotating, checklisting and portfolios. The most important aspect of assessment is that the tasks should align with the child's learning experiences, and they should be designed to provide all children with an opportunity to demonstrate what they know and can do.

External assessments
In the early years of schooling, there is often a focus on assessing children's mathematical capabilities to identify children who may be at risk in mathematics learning. Many education authorities use various specific assessments for these purposes. For example, a Year 2 diagnostic test may be used to map children's progress against a developmental numeracy continuum to identify children who require intervention and to provide additional support to these children (see Education Queensland 1998). Regardless of the authority that administers the assessment, the similarity in all early assessments of children's mathematics is that they are implemented by the children's usual classroom teacher and are undertaken individually (Department of Education and Early Childhood Development [DEECD] 2013).

A major research project conducted during the period 1999–2001 (The Early Years Numeracy Project) resulted in the identification of numeracy 'growth points' that are central to mathematical knowledge growth and development in the following topics: counting, place value, strategies for addition and subtraction, strategies for multiplication and division, time, length measurement framework, mass measurement framework, properties of shape and visualisation and orientation (DEECD 2013). Each of these topics is further broken into a series of between four and six growth points that indicate the level of children's development.

Conclusion

This chapter has overviewed mathematics teaching and learning in the first three years of schooling. As with the other chapters of this book, our intention is not to be prescriptive, but rather to provide advice and examples of how teachers might approach planning, design teaching and learning activities and assess children's mathematical knowledge and skills. Many of the activities can be adapted and used in other contexts and for other concepts. The next three chapters continue these ideas, firstly focusing on number and algebra in Chapter 10 and then on statistics and probability in Chapter 11, and geometry and measurement in Chapter 12.

10

Number and Algebra

Children have number and pattern knowledge before they come to school. From early play environments, mental mathematical structures have developed and children are receptive to new and novel tasks that formalise their mathematical knowledge. Children come to school very eager and keen to learn. It is worth noting that children generally do not exhibit signs and symptoms of anxiety about learning mathematics before the commencement of school. Yet fear of mathematics is a debilitating state that impacts children's self-concept as a learner and their self-confidence associated with their own capabilities for mathematics. As learning about number and 'doing sums' are generally most closely associated with children's perceptions of school mathematics, it is important for teachers to ensure that these topics in mathematics provide positive learning experiences for children.

In the past, approaches to school mathematics emphasised activities involving processes of identifying the attribute (find all the blue blocks), sorting, classifying, matching, patterning, comparing and ordering. Considerable time was devoted to these activities. It is now generally accepted that children learn these processes as a natural result of self-directed play. Many children spontaneously organise collections of objects—for example, a set of toy vehicles—according to various attributes: colour, number of wheels, type of vehicle (cars, trucks, motorbikes, tractors). They may line them up to create a pattern. They may display them in a semi-circle according to their own classification system, or match similar vehicles in pairs. This means that teachers do not need to spend a lot of time on activities to target these processes. Instead, the focus should be on number and patterning (patterning being an important first step in algebraic thinking).

Overview

This chapter addresses core number and patterning concepts and skills. A variety of teaching strategies can be used to aid this development. These range from capitalising on children's play, through guided questioning, to deliberately structuring learning environments incorporating number, to direct teaching approaches. Each of these methods has its own strengths, and teachers need to make informed decisions as to which strategies to use to best achieve their children's learning goals. A balanced approach is always best. While it is good teaching practice to capitalise on children's interests and activities to create productive learning episodes, it is also perfectly reasonable in some circumstances to adopt a more traditional approach, where children learn through watching, listening, answering questions, reasoning and practising (all legitimate and important active learner skills) as they are guided through an activity by the teacher. Therefore, the chapter incorporates examples of this balanced approach.

Number

Before children come to school, they are aware of number. They know how old they are, they know the number of their house, they know the number of their favourite football player and they know the number of their mother's work office. They may be able to count, but they may not be 'rational' counters.

Focus 1: Counting
Learning to count occurs in developmental stages, so if teachers are able to identify the child's learning stage, it will assist in planning for teaching. The three main stages of learning to count are rote counting, point counting and rational counting:

- *Rote counting* occurs when the child can say a sequence of number names and the sequence is very stable. Initially, the numbers may not be in the correct order or there may be missing numbers. For example, the child counts to 10 as follows: 1, 2, 3, 5, 7, 8, 10 and, when asked to repeat, the same sequence occurs.

- *Point counting* occurs when the child counts a collection of objects, typified by pointing at each object in turn. Initially, the child may state two or more numbers at each object. For example, for three items, the child may say the following: 'one, two' . . . 'three, four' . . . 'five'. If asked how many objects in total, the child will repeat the point counting and the sequence. Once a child has developed the skill of point counting, they use one-to-one correspondence, saying each number name once and without counting any object more than once (Frank 1989). The child may not be able to state how many objects are in the collection.
- *Rational counting* occurs when the child knows that counting must be done in order, the order of the items is irrelevant, and the last number tells how many in the collection.

> **Teaching point:** Ensure that children don't just say the number names but have as many varied opportunities as possible to count objects—especially objects that they can physical manipulate as they count. As children's competence and confidence grow, give them opportunities to count backwards as well as forwards. This is an important precursor to the development of understanding of addition and subtraction.

Growth points in counting

The Early Years Numeracy Research Project identified the growth points of children in counting (DEECD 2013). The first three major growth points in children's development of counting are:

- counting all in a collection
- counting on from a given number (e.g. count on 4 more from 9)
- counting back to (e.g. count back to 8 from 11) and back from (e.g. count back three numbers from 11) a particular number.

These particular growth points mean that children can build their understanding of number and number relationships through skip-counting activities.

Representations when counting

Ensure that children are provided with many opportunities to experience the verbal, physical (concrete) and symbolic representations of any mathematical concept. When developing understanding of number and counting, build conceptual understanding through the use of appropriate physical or diagrammatic representations of various numbers with written and verbal language and symbolic representations as illustrated in Figure 10.1:

Figure 10.1 Multiple representations of 3

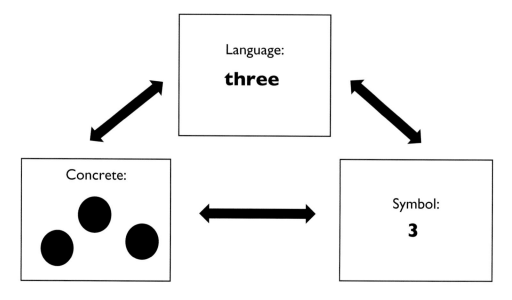

Make cards so that children can match the three modes such as those in Figure 10.2.

Figure 10.2 Sample cards with multiple representations of 3

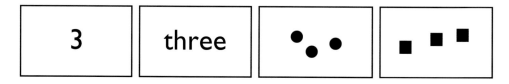

Find interesting ways of asking children to find, make and represent collections of various amounts:

- How many pencils in your tin at your desk?
- How many objects in your school bag?
- How many items in your lunchbox?
- How many people in your family?

It is possible to complete similar activities using ICT, such as apps for counting. However, the learning is more powerful if the child has an opportunity to complete the activity in the real world and then undertake further practice using the ICT.

Subitising

Young children have an innate sense of being able to determine the total of a collection without counting. This capacity is called subitising. Children have the capacity to subitise before they come to school. This innate capacity is often not capitalised upon as teachers emphasise the importance of touching objects while counting, or ask children to check how many in a collection when adding: '3 plus 4 is . . . let's count to check: 1, 2, 3, and 4, 5, 6, 7—yes, there are seven in this collection'. To celebrate and promote this innate capacity, include subitising activities on a regular basis. Put a collection of counter images on the IWB. 'Flash' the collection for a second and ask children how many there are in the collection. Experiment with various arrangements to see how they help or hinder accuracy. Ask children how they see the counters to determine the total and whether they actually mentally group the collection. If there are two sets of five counters on the screen and children can readily state that there are ten counters, they are already performing addition without having to count the whole collection. There are several apps available that are useful for developing the skill of subitising.

Focus 2: Extending counting

Skip counting

Once children are rational counters, make skip-counting a daily routine in the classroom. Just as they learn to recite rhymes, poems and songs, they will be able to recite number sequences. Even if the skip-counting pattern goes beyond children's conceptualisation of the size of the numbers, they will be able to continue the sequence with teacher support to notice patterns in various counting sequences.

> **Teaching point:** As a personal experiment to help you understand the process of developing fluency and competence, start with a number (e.g. 81) and count backwards aloud in 7s. You will find that the first time is quite challenging or slow. You may make mistakes. If you repeat the activity a number of times, you will find that your fluency and accuracy improve. This illustrates the importance of providing multiple learning opportunities for children.

Counting in tens

Provide children with bundling sticks and rubber bands. Every group of ten is held together with a rubber band. Children grasp each group of ten as they say the counting pattern: 10, 20, 30, 40 . . . As they get closer to 100, they will realise that there are too many to hold in their hand. This is a good way of building number sense of the size of 100. Count backwards from 100.

> **Teaching point:** Remember that, in the first three years of schooling, children will be at various developmental stages, and consequently the activities described must be tailored to suit the age and ability of all children.

Figure 10.3 Bundles of ten sticks

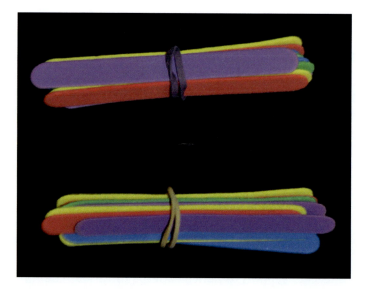

As children's counting skills develop, their counting can be extended beyond 100. Each child brings one group of ten to the mat. In a circle, each child holds up a bundle of ten as the counting commences in a circle. If there are 25 children in the class, the total will be 250. Count backwards commencing from the end-point (250).

If the children are ready, the activity can be extended to skip-counting in tens by starting at, for example, 13. The child who starts the count will have one bundle of ten and three loose items in front of them. All other children present their group of ten: 13, 23, 33, 43, 53 . . . All children are adding one group of ten to the count, while the child who began is the only one who has three extra bundling sticks to show the beginning number of 13.

Counting in fives
The children sit in a circle and one child is nominated to commence the count. That child raises first one hand and then the other as all children join the counting sequence: 5, 10. The second child then follows, but all continue with the count: 15, 20. This continues until all hands are raised and the total number of fingers in the room is identified. Count backwards from the total reached. Create a permanent record of counting in fives by children tracing around and cutting out a picture of their hands. They decorate the pictures, which are then displayed on a long piece of paper with the counting sequence written underneath.

Counting in twos
The children sit in a circle (as for counting in fives). This time, they blink their eyes for each number in the sequence. A wall chart can be created as children draw pictures of their eyes, or cut out pictures of eyes from people in magazines.

> **Teaching point:** With all counting activities, there are ICT resources for the IWB, computers and tablets that are excellent for developing visual and symbolic representations of numbers, and for reinforcement and consolidation; however, it is important that children have adequate physical experiences with counting.

Counting in 100s and 1 000s
As children learn the sequence of the numbers 1–10, using place value principles, they can later move on to learning to count in 100s or 1 000s as they are applying the sequence to a new group of numbers:

- Counting in 100s: 100, 200, 300, 400, 500 . . .
- Counting in 1 000s: 1 000, 2 000, 3 000, 4 000, 5 000 . . .

When skip-counting in 100s by applying the sequence of names for numbers 1–10, children will reach 1 000 after ten counts, which they may state as: 'ten hundred'. When skip counting in 1 000s, this is not the case, as there is no change of name at the point of 10 000 and in fact the sequence is easier than for 100s. In the early years of school, the teacher's role is to build understanding of the magnitude of 1 000 as appropriate according to the expectations of the curriculum. The size of 1 000 can be readily seen by examining the blocks in the Maths Attribute Blocks—ten ones make one ten, ten tens make 100, ten hundreds make 1 000. The introduction of new places in the place value system should also be a teaching focus, with connections made to the language, symbolic and visual/pictorial representations of large numbers.

Types of numbers
There are three types of numbers that children will encounter: cardinal, ordinal and nominal. It is not important for children to know these names, but it is important that teachers are aware of these three types of numbers and build children's understanding of them:

- *Cardinal* numbers tell 'how many'. When children are rational counters, they have the capacity to work with numbers in this way.
- *Ordinal* numbers relate to position: first, second, third, and their symbolic representation are 1st, 2nd, 3rd. Teachers can pose interesting questions for children to reflect on ordinal numbers, such as 'How can I be third and also last?'
- *Nominal* numbers have no 'value' but are associated with a particular situation. For example, racing cars, football players, telephone numbers and postcodes all use numbers, but they do not have an inherent number meaning. They are merely used for identification purposes.

Focus 3: Fraction foundations
Halving and doubling
The first fraction that children encounter is one-half. They are very familiar with dividing things into two parts to 'share', most often with siblings and friends. They will be used to having their toast or their sandwiches cut 'in half'. In their first year of school, children's intuitive understanding of halves is formalised to align with the mathematical concept of half as being one quantity of a collection divided into two equal parts. Through dividing collections and objects, the teacher connects the language and concrete representation to the symbolic (pictures of objects/collections divided into two equal parts; 'one-half'; $\frac{1}{2}$).

Activities for consolidating half include:

- pictures of various shapes to be divided into halves
- pictures of half objects where children need to draw the other half

NUMBER AND ALGEBRA   147

- groups of objects where children need to split them into two equal parts, labelling each group as 'half'
- connecting to finding lines of symmetry—splitting pictures into two equal pieces so that there is a mirror image
- finding letters of the alphabet that can be split in half to show a mirror image.

These activities can be supplemented using visuals on the IWB.

At the same time that numbers are being divided into halves, doubles can be introduced as the opposite action to halving: double 5 is 10; double 4 is 8; double 1 is 2. Maintain fluency in finding half and double by including such calculations in the daily mental computation exercises. To help children remember the doubles for the numbers 1–10, ask them to think of 'things' or objects that can be associated with each of those numbers, and then think of the total if there are two sets of those 'things':

1. stop sign, person, mouth, conductor's baton
2. drumsticks, bicycle wheels, eyes and ears
3. tricycle wheels
4. car wheels
5. fingers on a hand
6. insect legs
7. one week on a calendar
8. octopus tentacles
9. players in a softball/baseball team
10. squid tentacles.

Children create a mural to show these objects in twos. They make the connection that, for example, two tricycles have double three wheels—six wheels in total. This provides a visual image to which children can refer to assist in remembering doubles.

The empty number line: A tool for developing and consolidating concepts
An empty number line can be created using a piece of washing line and some pegs with which to attach number cards (see Figure 10.4). This is an invaluable resource for assisting children to develop conceptual understanding of number and properties of number through locating numbers on a number line. The empty number line can also be used to promote multiplicative thinking and number sense. Using various numbers on cards, the empty number line can extend from whole numbers to fractions, decimals, percentages and integers.

Figure 10.4 The string number line requires simple materials and is a versatile resource

It is a good idea to include the zero when working with the number line so that children become familiar with the location of zero and use it as a reference point. The procedure for using the number line for a whole-class demonstration is outlined below.

1. Nominate two volunteers to hold the line tight (change these regularly).
2. Peg the 0-card at the left end and the 2-card at the other. The left to right convention is important. Ensure all children sit in front of the number line.
3. Ask for another volunteer and provide them with the 1 card. Their task is to place the card in the appropriate place, but the rest of the class should be providing input as to where it should go. When there is general consensus that the card is located at the appropriate point, ask the children how they know and how they could check. Point out that the distance between the 0 and 1 should be the same as the distance between the 1 and 2.
4. The children holding the ends of the number line now assist in folding the number line so that the pegs at 0 and 2 meet. They then adjust the 1 card to be at the point of the fold.

Other sequences of numbers for the number line includes:

- Peg 0 and 4 locate 2
- Peg 0 and 6 locate 3
- Peg 0 and 8 locate 4

Note that the higher number is an even number, and the number to locate is half of that number. Consider the level of difficulty if providing an odd number as the higher number—for example, 3. The mid-point between 0 and 3 is $1\frac{1}{2}$, which is tricky if children have not learnt fractions. If they are trying to peg number 1 and 2 on the number line, the number line must be folded into thirds between 0 and 3 to locate each of these numbers. This is an extra level of difficulty.

> **Teaching point:** Where possible, ask the children to explain their actions and provide prompting questions to scaffold their thinking. The empty number line is an excellent assessment tool for teachers because it allows them to monitor the development of children's understanding of number.

To add more numbers to the number line, consider those examples that rely on halving in the first instance. For the example of Peg 0 and 8 locate 4, locating the numbers 2 and 6 will be a simpler process than if the children were locating 2 and 4 after pegging 0 and 6.

When appropriate, children's understanding of the number line can be extended by asking them to peg 0 and 100 on the number line. This requires the number line to be 'empty' so that children do not feel the need to extend the line itself, but to rescale the number line to represent a range of numbers other than the numbers between 0 and 10. Simple number examples are:

- Peg 0 and 100   locate 50; locate 25
- Peg 0 and 80   locate 40; locate 20
- Peg 0 and 200   locate 100; locate 50

Finding half as a mental computation strategy
Determining 'half' of an amount is a major mental computation strategy. This is the process in which children have engaged in the previous examples. As children learn about numbers, exploration of one-half of various amounts will be a natural extension. The same activities can be reworded to include the use of the word 'half':

- Peg 0 and 10   What is half of 10?   5 is half of 10
- Peg 0 and 4   What is half of 4?   2 is half of 4
- Peg 0 and 2   What is half of 2?   1 is half of 2

150 TEACHING EARLY YEARS MATHEMATICS, SCIENCE AND ICT

Fractions on the empty number line

Whole numbers are placed on the number line to build understanding of the magnitude of numbers and the appropriate way in which numbers should be represented on a number line. It is equally important to locate fractions on the number line. This shows the position of numbers between whole numbers and builds students' understanding of the way the number line can be scaled and rescaled to show numbers of focus. That is, if trying to locate $\frac{1}{2}$ on a number line, it is easier to see that it is halfway between 0 and 1 if 0 and 1 are the only two numbers on the number line before locating $\frac{1}{2}$, compared with a number line that shows, for example, 0 and 10.

As with activities for locating whole numbers on a number line, careful selection of specific fractions must occur to ensure children can see that the distance between the numbers is proportionally correct. A sequence of unit fractions (i.e. fractions whose numerator is 1) for the number line is as follows:

- Peg 0 and 1   locate $\frac{1}{2}$
- Peg 0 and 1   locate $\frac{1}{4}$

Exploring fractions that belong to the same 'family' (e.g., $\frac{1}{2}, \frac{1}{4}$) connects understanding of one-whole being divided into smaller parts, and that the larger the denominator, the smaller the parts in unit fractions.

> **Teaching point:** The empty number line is a simple tool that can be used effectively and efficiently throughout the year. It has numerous features that are beneficial for learning. For example, it is kinaesthetic and visual, and it requires children to collaborate and articulate their reasoning. It can also be self-correcting.

Focus 4: Place value

An understanding of place value is fundamental to knowing number and number relationships. Lack of place value understanding is frequently cited as the key issue associated with children's learning difficulties in mathematics. As children work with numbers greater than 10, they begin to build understanding of place value in the way that numbers are represented. As children make different numbers using bundling sticks or MAB, connect the symbolic representation with the physical representation using a place value chart like that shown in Figure 10.5.

Figure 10.5 Place value chart showing 43

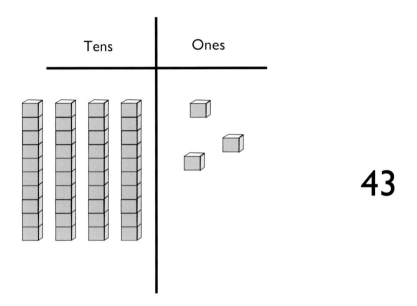

Place value is about grouping and regrouping. Exploration of various ways in which collections can be grouped to support counting strengthens place value understanding. The following Chicken scramble and Packaging Cubi-jubes activities are examples of investigative tasks that promote grouping and regrouping.

Chicken scramble
Provide each group of children with a packet of shell, spiral or elbow pasta. Ask them to estimate the number of pieces of pasta in the packet. The pasta is placed in the middle of the table and the children are asked to count how many pieces of pasta were in the packet. This is done by having the children take one piece of pasta at a time, as quickly as possible (hence the name 'scramble'). As each child's collection grows, the pasta pieces are arranged in groups of ten. Once all the pasta has been collected, each child has to indicate how much pasta they have, perhaps by writing the amount symbolically. The final step is for the children to work together to determine the total number of pasta pieces in the packet. This process may require some regrouping. For example, if Amit has 17 pieces and Eloise has 25 pieces, between them they will initially have three groups of ten, a group of seven, and a group of five. The groups of five and seven can be regrouped to make

another group of ten with two left over, so the result is four groups of ten plus two, making a total of 42. Make sure that their pasta count is verified before the pasta is returned to the packet.

This activity gives children hands-on experience with place value and grouping. It is particularly beneficial in aiding the move from concrete to symbolic if children are given opportunities to record their numbers. It can also be viewed as an addition activity. The idea of the scramble is that each child has different amounts. The scramble can be repeated to illustrate that while each child has different numbers of pasta pieces each time, the total remains the same.

Figure 10.6 Two children's pasta collections showing 21 and 13 pieces of pasta respectively

Packaging Cubi-jubes
A new sweet has been created that is shaped like a cube. It has been named a Cubi-jube. Cubi-jubes are wrapped into packs of ten and the wrapper is bright and colourful. For transport from the sweet factory to the shop, the packets of ten Cubi-jubes are packed in boxes of ten. (Therefore, there are ten Cubi-jubes in a pack and 10 x 10 Cubi-jubes in a box.) They are displayed on shop counters and shelves in their open box.

The children are asked to make the individual packs of ten Cubi-jubes and then create a box of ten packs of ten. Provide children with appropriate material to replicate the packaging of Cubi-jubes, such as multilink or unifix blocks, coloured paper, sticky tape and rulers. The emphasis is placed on the groups of one Cubi-jube, ten Cubi-jubes in a pack and 100 Cubi-jubes in a box. This should be connected to place value of ones, tens and hundreds. The concrete representations should be related to the symbolic. Once the children have made their packs and boxes, they can role-play scenarios in which they buy and sell their Cubi-jubes. This provides exposure to adding and grouping activities. For example, if I buy three packs of Cubi-jubes, I have 30 Cubi-jubes in total. If I buy a box and two packs, I have 120 Cubi-jubes. If I buy two packs and eat three Cubi-jubes, I have one pack of ten and seven single Cubi-jubes, making a total of 17.

> **Teaching point:** In the previous two activities, children can be encouraged to use grouping and partitioning to make their counting easier. For example, arranging in groups of ten and counting the groups is easier than counting individual items. Remember that the focus of these activities is to build children's understanding of place value. As often as possible, they should be recording the numbers symbolically. The teacher should draw children's attention to the place value column location of each number.

Focus 5: Money and financial mathematics

Activities involving money provide many opportunities to engage children in rich number experiences and exciting learning environments. For example, when a shop is set up in the classroom, a play-based environment is created where children can learn coin identification and counting change, which involves knowing coins and their combinations. They can also be involved in developing personal financial plans, where they earn 'money' for the shop based on activities in the classroom and they plan for purchasing particular items at the shop. Children can keep simple 'bankbooks' to keep track of the 'money' they earn and how much they spend. When children have the skills, this activity can also be recorded using appropriate software. They can make predictions about how many weeks it may take them to save enough money for a large purchase.

> **Teaching point:** Teachers need to adapt and add activities according to their curriculum and depending on their currency. For example, in some cases the size of coins is not relative to their value (e.g. the Australian $2 coin is smaller than the $1 coin). Children also need experience in ordering coins according to their value. Activities involving money can provide further opportunities for practising skills such as skip-counting and building ideas about counting on and back (when paying and giving change). These activities are also good for place value and later for use as the basis for working with decimals.

Money clumps

Learning about coins and their value is an opportunity to enhance children's early multiplicative thinking. Create a set of large cards and glue a proportionally sized picture of various coins (one coin on each card) on the cards. Ensure there are enough cards for all children in the class.

Through the activity of *money clumps*, children will experience grouping and regrouping. That is, $2 \times 5c$ coins have the same total as $1 \times 10c$ and so on. Clear a space in the classroom so that children can move. Play some music and get children to 'dance' gently around the room. When the teacher stops the music, an instruction is given—for example: 'Make $1.00'. The children have to quickly find groups of coins to add to the given amount. The various instructions given by the teacher can be 'inclusive' of all coins (e.g. 'Make $2.00') or very selective (e.g. 'Make 20c with only four coins').

Focus 6: Early addition and subtraction

Early addition and subtraction begins with modelling situations using concrete materials and then making connections between the operation and the symbolic representation of the situation. Children need to be exposed to a range of addition and subtraction situations and problems to build understanding of the operation rather than relying solely on key words associated with addition and subtraction, such as add, altogether, join and sum for addition, and take away, leave, remove and subtract for subtraction. Essentially, addition problems involve two given parts with the object of determining the whole. For subtraction problems, the whole and one of the parts is given and the object is to determine the other part. There are four main types of addition and subtraction problems: joining, inaction, comparison and take away, as seen in Table 10.1.

The problem types in Table 10.1 don't need to be presented formally to children; the examples are provided to illustrate the range of ways in which addition and subtraction scenarios can be presented to children.

Focus 7: Early multiplication and division

Conceptual understanding of multiplication and division is the beginning point of multiplicative thinking. Multiplicative thinking is an essential component of proportional reasoning, which is required for successful operation in many mathematical topics later in school (such as fractions, decimals, percentages, rates, ratios) and other topics in the curriculum (e.g. time lines in history, speed in science, body proportions in art).

NUMBER AND ALGEBRA   155

Table 10.1 Addition and subtraction problem types

Problem type	Addition 2 + 3 = 5 part + part = whole	Subtraction 5 − 3 = 2 whole − part = part
Join	Two ducks on the pond. Three more came to join them. How many altogether?	Five ducks on the pond after three ducks had flown in to join them. How many ducks were there before the arrival of the new ducks?
Inaction	Two ducks swimming on the pond; three ducks sitting under the trees. How many ducks altogether at the pond?	Five ducks at the pond; two swimming on the water, the others sitting under the tree. How many are under the tree?
Comparison	Two ducks on the first pond and three more ducks on the second pond compared to the first pond. How many ducks on the second pond?	Five ducks on the first pond and three fewer ducks on the second pond. How many ducks are at the second pond?
Take-away	Two ducks on the pond after three ducks had flown away. How many ducks were there to start with?	Five ducks at the pond. Three flew away. How many ducks at the pond now?

Multiplicative situations

Multiplicative situations can be introduced in a number of ways:

- *Grouping:* Five sweets per bag; three bags. How many sweets altogether?
- *Rate:* Candy canes cost 5c each. How much will three cost?
- *Scalar:* Jan has three times as many cards as Ruby. Ruby has five cards. How many does Jan have?
- *Cross-product:* Three different shirts (red, orange, yellow) and two different shorts (brown, black). How many different outfit combinations?

Grouping problems are the most commonly used problems to which children are exposed in school. It is important that they are also exposed to all other types. If there is a 'shop' in the classroom, rate questions could be posed in authentic contexts. Also, children should be encouraged to use simple proportional reasoning strategies to solve such problems as they model the equivalent situations:

1 candy cane	5c
2 candy canes	10c
3 candy canes	15c

This type of representation is extremely valuable for future proportion situations where the two quantities are related in a multiplicative sense and the solution strategy maintains the relationship through the 'repeated addition' approach. Rate problems can be modelled in the same way.

Cross-product multiplication situations are difficult for children. They need to be provided with hands-on activities to assist them to see the relationship between the number of options and the solution (three shirts; two shorts; $3 \times 2 = 6$ possible combinations). Create sets of cards with the different options on each card. The task is for children to use logical thinking to create all different outfits/combinations without repeats. In the card set, ensure that there are more pieces than required so that children are cued to check whether they have repeated any combinations. This activity links to some commercially published books that show 'crazy animals' where there are three different types of heads, three different types of bodies and three different types of legs. The pages in the book are cut at each section of the animal so different 'crazy' animals can be created (e.g. an animal that has a dog head, a mouse body and duck feet). If left as a book, there is little chance that children will make the connection between the number of different parts and the total number of possible animals. Using separate cards for the crazy animal activity can be more helpful for children to account for the possible combinations, and they are more likely to reflect on the process they used to achieve the solution. Activities such as these can also be completed using software, apps and the IWB. Children may enjoy creating their own crazy animals to share with their classmates. Examples of crazy animals created using a computer are shown in Figure 10.7.

When there are three different heads, three different bodies, and three different types of legs, there are $3 \times 3 \times 3 = 27$ different possible combinations. This is likely to be too challenging for some young children. Using three animals and two body parts would lead to a simpler set of solutions.

Arrays
Arrays are a common representation of multiplication situations, yet for many children, arrays are not readily recognised in this way. To build children's understanding of arrays, provide them with multiplication situations that can be represented with concrete materials in an array. For example, for a meeting, the teacher asks

NUMBER AND ALGEBRA 157

Figure 10.7 Crazy animals made from (a) three and (b) two body parts

the children to organise the chairs into three rows, with five chairs in each row. A diagram such as that in Figure 10.8 can be used to help the children visualise the situation.

Figure 10.8 Diagram of three rows of five chairs

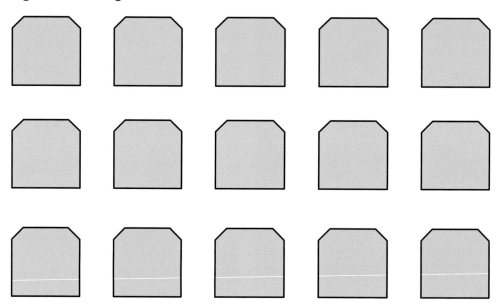

The teacher's role is to draw children's attention to the total (15) and the number of chairs in each row and column (3 × 5). Encourage children to find pictures or objects in arrays in the real world that they can bring to the classroom and display—for example, seedling punnets at the gardening store will be in arrays. Other examples include an egg carton (2 × 6), a muffin tray (2 × 3) and packets of biscuits. Don't forget to include arrays that involve objects multiplied by 1.

Division problems
There are two main types of division problems: partition and quotition division:

- *Partition division*: Share the packet of twelve sweets equally among four people. The action is sharing or dealing (one for you, one for you, one for you, etc.). The number of groups (4) is known, but the number in each group is not known.

Figure 10.9 Real world examples of arrays: (a) building windows (3 × 4); (b) muffin pan (3 × 2); (c) chest of drawers (3 × 1); (d) egg carton (2 × 3)

160   TEACHING EARLY YEARS MATHEMATICS, SCIENCE AND ICT

- *Quotition division*: There are twelve sweets in this packet. Each person is to be given three each. With how many people can you share this packet of lollies? The action is grouping into threes, but the total number of groups of three is not known.

Patterning: The basis of algebra

Children notice patterns in their environment. They will study printed fabric to see where the pattern repeats. They will explore tiles on the floor to notice the patterns that are shown. They will see patterns in wallpaper. If children don't notice such patterns in their environment, bring them to their attention. Digital cameras and a field excursion around the school will result in some great patterns to be shared. Copying and extending patterns is the basis of algebraic thinking.

Some physical patterning ideas include:

- Create two-element (A B A B . . .) and three-element (A B C A B C . . .) patterns with a variety of materials, including children themselves:
  - with pattern blocks (square, circle, square, circle . . .)
  - with numbers (1 2 1 2 1 2 . . .)
  - with actions (snap, stomp, snap, stomp . . .)
  - with children (sit, stand, sit, stand . . .)

Use the IWB for visualising and sharing patterns and to discuss patterns:

- Create more challenging patterns that involve repeating some elements:
  - red, red, blue, red, red, blue . . .
  - big square, big square, small square, big square, big square, triangle, big square, big square, small square . . .
- Extend the pattern by changing one of the elements:
  - (blue) square, square, circle, (red) square, square, circle, (yellow) square, square, circle . . .

It is also important to examine the relationship between an element in a pattern and its position in that pattern. In a two-element pattern, A B A B A B . . ., draw the children's attention to the fact that the first, third and fifth elements are 'A', and the second, fourth and sixth elements are 'B'. Ask them to predict what the eighth element will be: A or B. For older children, ask them to predict what the tenth element might be. Ask them to generalise about the position and the element. This becomes more of a challenge in more complex repeating patterns, but as long

NUMBER AND ALGEBRA 161

as the pattern can be repeated, the generalisation can be made. In the example above of: big square, big square, small square, big square, big square, triangle, big square, big square, small square . . . it is easy to see that after every two big squares there will be either a small square or a triangle. However, in the last example given above, where the colour changes, children have little idea of what the next colour might be unless there has been some predetermined sequence that will be used. This means that when asking children to generalise from the given pattern, the pattern must have been repeated enough times to ensure that it is actually a repeating pattern. Although children may find this activity difficult, it is worth the time to allow children to consider how to generalise from patterns at every opportunity.

As an extension activity, the children can be asked to make their own patterns to share with the class. Their classmates can be asked to make predictions or answer questions posed by the maker of the pattern or the teacher. Patterns can be made using numbers, shapes or physical objects, or they can be made using the IWB or a computer.

Focus 1: Exploring number patterns
As children skip-count in various intervals, they are building their understanding of the relationships between numbers. They are learning about factors, multiples and divisibility rules. Provide children with time to explore these relationships. For example, when counting in fives: 5 10 15 20 25 30 35 40 45 50 . . . , the multiples of 5 are generated. It can also be readily seen that each number ends in 5 or 0. This means that for a number to be divisible by 5, it must end in a five or zero. It also means that one of its factors will be 5.

For older children, use the 99 board to explore number patterns. Select an interval to count in, and then use unifix blocks or transparent counters to cover each multiple of that number. Similar activities can be completed using tablets and apps or the IWB. Start with the obvious and simple visual patterns and look at how the blocks are displayed on the board:

- *Count in tens.* The blocks make a straight line down the board as all numbers ending in zero are covered.
- *Count in fives.* A new strip of blocks appears on the board along with all the tens.
- *Count in twos.* The blocks do not cover numbers previously covered when counting in fives, except for the line of multiples of ten.
- *Count in nines.* An interesting diagonal pattern emerges, as in Figure 10.10.

162 TEACHING EARLY YEARS MATHEMATICS, SCIENCE AND ICT

Figure 10.10 A 99 board showing the pattern when counting in nines

0	1	2	3	4	5	6	7	8	9
10	11	12	13	14	15	16	17	18	19
20	21	22	23	24	25	26	27	28	29
30	31	32	33	34	35	36	37	38	39
40	41	42	43	44	45	46	47	48	49
50	51	52	53	54	55	56	57	58	59
60	61	62	63	64	65	66	67	68	69
70	71	72	73	74	75	76	77	78	79
80	81	82	83	84	85	86	87	88	89
90	91	92	93	94	95	96	97	98	99

- *Count in fours.* Every second line repeats. This is a well-ordered and structured pattern. Note the pattern of the digit in the ones place when counting in fours: 4, 8, 2, 6, 0, 4, 8, 2, 6, 0.
- *Count in eights.* This is a natural extension of counting in fours, as it involves removing blocks that were originally on the board for counting in fours.
- *Count in threes.* This makes a very exciting pattern on the board, but also shows the difficulty of the threes pattern before it begins to repeat itself.
- *Count in sixes.* Like counting in eights, this is a natural extension of counting in threes as it involves removing blocks that were originally on the board for counting in threes.
- *Count in sevens.* This is a tricky pattern, and one that is difficult to skip count. Displaying it on the 99 board shows how long it takes before the pattern repeats.

Teaching point: Children in the first three years are not expected to skip-count in all the increments mentioned in this example. These activities assume that the children have access to a 99 board, whether physically or on the IWB, to support them in their use of counting-on strategies.

Rainbow numbers

Some classrooms display rainbow numbers where the sequence 1, 2, 3, 4, 5, 6, 7, 8, 9, 10 is presented with lines drawn between 1 and 10, 2 and 9, 3 and 8, etc., to show how these all add to 11. An example is shown in Figure 10.11.

Figure 10.11 Rainbow numbers for 1 to 10

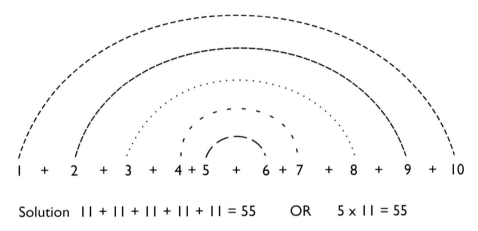

Teaching point: Thinking of how a counting sequence of numbers is related in this way is attributed to a mathematician named Gauss, who was said to have astonished his teacher by being able to calculate the sum of numbers from 1 to 100 (that is, 1 + 2 + 3 ... 98 + 99 + 100) in seconds. He applied the rainbow number process to do this. Think about the rainbow sequence for the numbers 1 to 10. There are ten counting numbers. There are five pairs of numbers that each total 11. That means that if we know how many counting numbers, we just need to divide that by two and then multiply by the total for each pair. The total for 1 + 2 + ... 9 + 10 is 5 × 11, which equals 55. For the numbers 1 to 100, there are 50 pairs of numbers that each add to 101. That means that the total is 50 × 101 = 5 050. Seeing this pattern means that any number sequence can be presented and the total can readily be determined. As children become familiar with numbers up to 10, 100 or 1 000, depending on their readiness, they can apply this thinking.

Focus 2: Function machines

Function machines are a novel way of getting children to 'guess my rule'. There are many function machines available on the internet, which can be programmed from simple to more challenging. However, a teacher can also create a simple function machine by drawing a box with a funnel going in and a funnel going out. Eyes and a mouth can also be added to bring character to the function machine. The teacher creates a table on the board that records particular numbers that 'go in' to the function machine and the number that 'comes out'. Children suggest input numbers until a pattern is established. They can then try to state the rule that describes the pattern (i.e. the function) that has been applied to each incoming number to produce the corresponding outgoing number.

Figure 10.12   A function machine sample problem

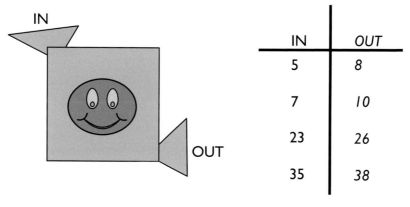

(Rule: add 3)

Teaching point: Function machines can also be used to help children move from additive thinking to multiplicative thinking. Where the example is 4 in and 8 out, 5 in and 10 out, they may initially think the first example is additive (4 + 4 = 8) but the addition of 4 doesn't work for the second example because when 5 goes in the result is not 9. This prompts the children to consider a doubling (multiplicative) situation: 4 × 2 = 8 and 5 × 2 = 10.

Basic facts of addition and multiplication

Methods of teaching and learning number facts have been a source of educational debate for many years. Purely transmissive teaching and rote learning, which traditionally were used to learn number facts, often led to children knowing an answer but having little if any understanding of the process. Alternatively, trying to teach all number facts purely through play-based, discovery or activity-based learning is neither sufficient nor efficient. Therefore, teachers should always look for opportunities to engage children in learning the basic facts through active learning environments and authentic situations when possible. At the same time, they should not be afraid to strengthen this learning through more structured means. A practical way is to expose the children to experiences via ICT or physical manipulatives, and then use symbolic representations and language to describe the operation.

When children learn their basic facts of addition and multiplication, not only are they learning valuable facts that are the basis for mental computation, but they are actually learning the laws for arithmetic, which are foundational to algebra. The commutative law cuts down the number of facts to be learned and remembered because once one fact is learned, its 'spin-around' is also known. For example, 3 + 6, start with the 6 and count on three more, rather than trying to count on 6 from a starting point of 3. The associative law is invoked in mental computation to make addition or multiplication simpler. For example, adding 7 + 8 + 3 may use the strategy of adding 7 and 3 first, as this is a readily recognised combination to 10, and then adding 8. The associative law allows flexibility in choosing where to begin rather than attempting to work from left to right. After learning basic facts and practising to automaticity, they should be applied to mental computation exercises on a regular basis. Without specifically learning the laws of arithmetic, children will become aware of how these laws assist in mental computation. Many software games are available for children to practise number facts and associated activities. Effective games allow children to move from level to level, and allow the teacher to have input into the activities. Games like these are great for consolidation and improving speed and accuracy.

Research shows that children's growth points associated with counting incorporate particular types of addition facts (DEECD 2013). After the development of rational counting, the next major growth point is being able to count on and back from a given number, followed by doubles, adding 10 to a given number, and knowing the combinations of numbers that total 10. Children use these strategies to learn their basic facts of addition. The next major growth point is being able to 'derive' solutions to new addition facts by accessing 'known' facts such as near doubles, adding 9, building 10 and fact families. This research supports a strategies approach to teaching basic facts, as outlined in this section. In engaging in a strategies approach, the teacher should look for multiple interesting and diverse activities and scenarios through which to do this.

166 TEACHING EARLY YEARS MATHEMATICS, SCIENCE AND ICT

A strategies approach to the basic addition facts

There are 121 basic facts of addition (0 + 0 . . . 10 + 10) that children need to learn to automaticity. Children need to be provided with ample time to learn the strategy and then, through varied and supportive practice as basic facts associated with each strategy become automatic, they become the basis for learning more facts.

The sequence is as follows:

- count-on facts—count on 1, 2, 3, 0
- doubles
- adding ten
- tens facts
- bridging ten
- near doubles.

Count-on facts—count on 1, 2, 3, 0

Counting-on is a valuable strategy that is used for mental computation of amounts beyond basic facts. However, children must be taught that the count-on strategy is only suitable for counting on amounts of 1, 2, 3 or 0. If used for amounts greater than that, there is more chance of error. When children start to use the count-on strategy, potential errors occur at the first instance as they count the first collection and then use the name of that collection as the first count. For example, when adding 6 and 2, they may say '6, 7', with the resulting answer being 7 rather than 8. This may stem from the fact that 6 and 2 have been represented to them in concrete form (six counters and two counters), with children feeling the need to count the original 6. This error also stems from looking at these numbers on a ruler (that is, locating the position of the 6 and then using 6 as the first number counted followed by the 7. To avoid this misconception, ensure that the total of the first number is held constant and the counting on commences with the next number (e.g. 6 + 2 means 7, 8 so the answer is 8). Using marbles in a tin and creating a noise can assist (see Figure 10.13).

Provide practice in having children circle the biggest number, and then count on. Counting on with zero is a special teaching point, as this is an addition situation where the total is unchanged. This is another arithmetic law that is foundational to algebra: The identity law means that when a zero is added to a number, the number remains unchanged.

Figure 10.13 A counting on strategy

Place 6 marbles in the tin but don't let children count them. Tell them, "there are 6 marbles in this tin"; drop in two more, one at a time, emphasizing the counting on: "... 7 ... 8"

Doubles and adding 10
Activities for helping children learn doubles to 10 were outlined earlier in this chapter. Similarly, adding 10 to numbers has also been outlined in the discussion of skip-counting in 10s. When focusing on basic addition facts, the teacher's role is to build connections between these activities and to ensure that children know the basic facts that belong to this category.

Tens facts
Tens facts are those numbers that add together to make 10. These facts are one of the most commonly used strategies for mental computation as it is a natural instinct to look for combinations that add to 10. For example, if adding 7, 6 and 3, many people would add the 7 and 3 first as a combination of 10. To assist children to connect and recognise combinations to 10, a ten frame and counters of two different colours are used, as shown in Figure 10.14.

Figure 10.14 A ten frame illustrating 7 + 3

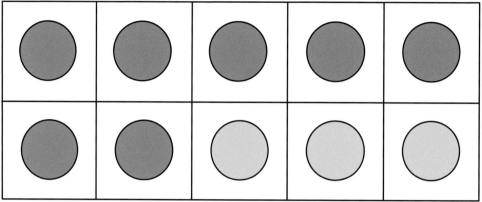

Bridging 10
The bridging 10 strategy is used for numbers that are close to 10, such as 9 and 8. Use a double ten frame to show why 9 + 4 is 10 + 3, as shown in Figure 10.15. Children readily see that the top frame only needs one more counter to be filled, so if one is taken from the bottom frame, we can see how this helps to learn bridging 10 facts.

Figure 10.15 A double ten frame to illustrate 9 + 4 = 10 + 3

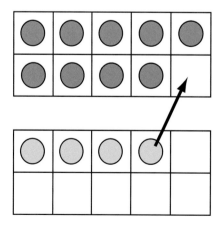

9 + 4 is the same as 10 + 3

Near doubles
Recognising near doubles is another useful strategy for mental computation. For example, to add 25 and 27, many people may readily recognise that this is the same as doubling 25 and adding two more. For teaching the near doubles strategy, use two different-coloured counters. Display both numbers to see how the fact is, for example, doubles plus 1. Grid paper will keep the counters in order and make comparison easier. This idea is shown in Figure 10.16.

Figure 10.16   Counters can be used to illustrate near doubles

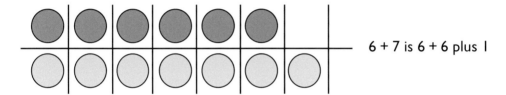

6 + 7 is 6 + 6 plus 1

All 121 addition facts mastered
Through using a strategies approach, facts are grouped according to the particular strategy that can be applied to assist in learning and then memorised. By using a 'fact grid', each category of facts can be coloured as they are encountered, providing a visual record of facts that have been learned and facts that are yet to be mastered. By referring to the grid, specific examples of facts that fall into a category can be identified, and these provide guidance as to the examples to use when exemplifying the strategy. For example, when demonstrating the doubles plus one and doubles plus 2 strategies, facts that have not been learned before include: 5 + 6 and 5 + 7, as well as 6 + 7 and 6 + 8. These facts would be most suitable for demonstrating this strategy, rather than previously learned facts such as 3 + 4, which is a count-on fact.

Individual fact grids can be a great assessment tool. When children maintain their own fact grid, they are engaging in self-assessment. The teacher can also use them to record children's mastery of the addition facts.

Fact families and learning subtraction facts
Once all the addition facts have been learned and practised to mastery, it is a simple task to learn subtraction facts. The strategy for subtraction facts is to 'think addition'. For example, to determine the solution to 12 − 7, think: 7 + what is 12? The child knows that 7 and 5 make 12, so 12 − 7 is 5. Subtraction facts link to 'fact

170   TEACHING EARLY YEARS MATHEMATICS, SCIENCE AND ICT

families'. Once again, a balance is needed to ensure that children understand these processes. Introduction and practice of subtraction facts should involve multiple experiences, including those in which the children use manipulatives or are engaged in problem-solving—for example, using the IWB.

Through exploration of associated subtraction facts, children become adept at identifying fact triples—that is, three numbers that are connected through the operations of addition and subtraction. Following on from the above example, the three numbers 12, 5, and 7 share a special relationship. There are actually four number facts that can be derived from these three numbers:

$$5 + 7 = 12$$
$$7 + 5 = 12$$
$$12 - 5 = 7$$
$$12 - 7 = 5$$

Knowing number families is a major growth point in the development of counting (DEECD 2013).

Basic facts of multiplication and division

A strategies approach to the basic multiplication facts

While formal learning of multiplication and division facts is usually not expected in the first three years of schooling, children can be prepared for this important step through activities discussed in this chapter, such as arrays, repeated addition and skip counting. As with the addition facts, multiplication facts are grouped according to a thinking strategy to support their recall. The order is:

- the easy facts—tens, fives, twos, ones
- the pattern facts—nines, fours, square numbers
- the last facts.

> **Teaching point:** If, in the early years, a teacher makes the decision to explore multiplication facts, the focus should be restricted to tens, fives, twos, and ones, which have been informally met already through skip-counting and doubling.

The easy facts: tens, fives, twos, ones
The grid in Figure 10.17 indicates the 'easy facts' with shading.

Figure 10.17 Number grid illustrating the easy facts: tens, fives, twos and ones

	0	1	2	3	4	5	6	7	8	9	10
0	0x0	0x1	0x2	0x3	0x4	0x5	0x6	0x7	0x8	0x9	0x10
1	1x0	1x1	1x2	1x3	1x4	1x5	1x6	1x7	1x8	1x9	1x10
2	2x0	2x1	2x2	2x3	2x4	2x5	2x6	2x7	2x8	2x9	2x10
3	3x0	3x1	3x2	3x3	3x4	3x5	3x6	3x7	3x8	3x9	3x10
4	4x0	4x1	4x2	4x3	4x4	4x5	4x6	4x7	4x8	4x9	4x10
5	5x0	5x1	5x2	5x3	5x4	5x5	5x6	5x7	5x8	5x9	5x10
6	6x0	6x1	6x2	6x3	6x4	6x5	6x6	6x7	6x8	6x9	6x10
7	7x0	7x1	7x2	7x3	7x4	7x5	7x6	7x7	7x8	7x9	7x10
8	8x0	8x1	8x2	8x3	8x4	8x5	8x6	8x7	8x8	8x9	8x10
9	9x0	9x1	9x2	9x3	9x4	9x5	9x6	9x7	9x8	9x9	9x10
10	10x0	10x1	10x2	10x3	10x4	10x5	10x6	10x7	10x8	10x9	10x10

Strategic thinking for the easy facts is as follows:

- *Tens*: Link to skip-counting in tens. Refresh the children's memory of making bundles of ten with paddle pop sticks and picking up each set of 10 while skip counting (10, 20, 30 . . .). If I have seven bundles of ten, how many sticks are there?
- *Fives*: Link to skip-counting using an analogue clock face—when the big hand is pointing to the 3, this is fifteen minutes (3×5).
- *Twos*: Think doubles—think of something that exists in a given amount (e.g., an octopus has eight tentacles; two octopuses have double eight tentacles, which means sixteen tentacles in total).
- *Ones*: These relate to arrays. Discussions with visual or physical representations can assist—such as 'If I have one lot of three, I still have three—the amount doesn't change; whereas if I have two lots of three, I have six.' Children can also use a calculator to verify the multiplication property of 1: any number $\times$ 1 is itself.

Conclusion

This chapter has focused on strategies for developing children's understanding of number, developing early number sense, and the use of patterning as a means of building the foundational understandings that will prepare children for later work in number and algebra. The emphasis is on the development of children's understanding of mathematical concepts and their use of mathematical language and representations. A range of ways to represent and communicate mathematical ideas has been presented. Teachers play a critical role in helping children make connections between the different ideas and concepts they encounter in mathematics, and in finding patterns and identifying relationships in the world around them.

Planning and reflection

Use the Planning and Reflection for Teaching template in Chapter 1 to more deeply consider and make personal decisions about the pedagogy, curriculum and assessment possibilities or requirements for this unit.

11

Statistics and Probability

This chapter provides ideas and teaching points about promoting young children's understanding of mathematical concepts associated with statistics and probability (often referred to as chance and data). Although statistics and probability are conceptually separate, teaching activities presented in this chapter frequently address these two aspects together, as working with data can help children build an understanding of chance concepts. The ideas presented are springboards that can be used to introduce key ideas to first-time learners or as consolidation and revision activities for children who may have been introduced to these topics in previous years. This strand of mathematics in the first three years of schooling is quite limited in scope when compared with the strands of Number & Algebra and Geometry & Measurement. Nevertheless, there are very important concepts and skills associated with this strand, and it offers many exciting and authentic opportunities for learning mathematics. It is particularly easy and important to use the concepts in statistics and probability in authentic contexts, such as in science or geography.

Young children are very familiar with the language of probability or chance from an early age. They know that when their parents say they 'might' be able to do something, then there is chance that the event will happen. However, there are also misconceptions about chance events that children bring with them to school, such as the chance of rolling a six on a die, which never seems to happen when

174 TEACHING EARLY YEARS MATHEMATICS, SCIENCE AND ICT

you need a six to start a board game. Conducting simple probability experiments and collecting data (statistics) assist in developing children's understanding of probability and provide a platform for talking about the language of probability. In such contexts, statistics and probability are interconnected, and this approach allows the teacher to focus on developing conceptual understanding of both areas within this strand of the mathematics curriculum.

EPISODE I

Developing an understanding of chance events

Certain and impossible events

Place a collection of objects (toy truck, small doll, golf ball) into a 'feely bag' as the children watch. Display the words 'certain' and 'impossible' on cards. As the teacher asks questions, the children point to the appropriate word.

*   Is there a toy truck in this bag?
*   Is there an elephant in this bag?
*   Is there a small doll in this bag?
*   Is there a soccer ball in this bag?

Check by tipping the objects out on to the table. Change the objects in the bag.

Using a two-outcome spinner

Using light cardboard with a matchstick (not a match) through the middle, make spinners that have only two outcomes. A square divided into two parts and coloured in two different colours can work well for this. As the square is spun, there are four edges upon which it can land, but there is an equal chance that it will land on either colour. Create a simple table as shown in Figure 11.1 to record the outcomes so that children can keep a tally of the number of times the spinner lands on either colour.

Explore the data that are collected. What colour will the spinner land on next? Why? There will be many instances when the actual outcomes won't match the expected outcomes, so it is important to collect sufficient data to ensure that appropriate conclusions are reached.

> **Teaching point:** At this age, many children will have difficulty understanding that each event is independent—that is, the next spin is not dependent upon the outcome of the previous spin, and there is an equal chance of either colour being the outcome. The important thing is that children have had the opportunity to explore and immerse themselves in these big concepts of chance. With further and varied exploration, they will develop appropriate concepts associated with chance events.

Figure 11.1 (a) Cardboard spinner and (b) tally table

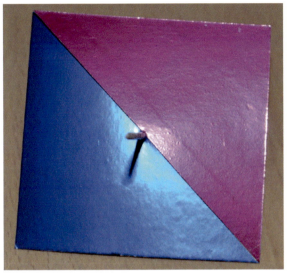

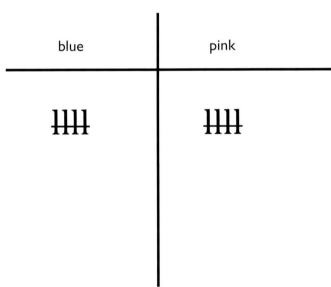

176   TEACHING EARLY YEARS MATHEMATICS, SCIENCE AND ICT

EPISODE 2

Working with data

In the simple spinner experiment outlined above, the children were collecting, organising, representing, analysing and interpreting data. Sometimes it can seem that data-collection activities are carried out for the sole purpose of representing the data on a graph. Too often, there is little discussion about data and what sorts of questions they might be used to answer. Data collection activities are much more valuable learning experiences when the data are collected for a purpose by ensuring that children are provided with authentic situations in which to collect real data. There are many opportunities for authentic data collection, interpretation and representation in science. This also provides a great opportunity to make links to the nature of science, since these activities are at the heart of scientists' work. The use of ICT can provide excellent means of collecting, organising, presenting and interpreting data.

Some interesting questions that can be posed to children to provide a meaningful context for data collection might include:

* What are the most common birds in our school?
* What sorts of insects live in our school?
* How busy is the road in front of our school?
* Who has the healthiest lunch?
* Which class makes the most litter?
* Would 'hot-dog Friday' be popular with students in our school?

The nature of these questions suggests their value in developing children's critical thinking about issues that affect them. The data collected to answer these questions can be used to make decisions or draw conclusions. Children can be encouraged to pose their own questions. Through collecting such data, children are engaging with important considerations when dealing with the collection of statistics—for example, they must consider what kind of data will help to answer the question or how many children should be surveyed to ensure that the result is valid.

> **Teaching point:** Just as it is important to understand the purposes of collecting data, their collection also provides opportunities to discuss with children that when we collect different data for different purposes, we can use different kinds of representations (e.g. bar graphs, tables, lists, picture graphs).

Children collecting data about themselves: Data angels

Provide children with an 'angel' template (see Figure 11.2) and ask them to decorate it as appropriate.

Figure 11.2 Data angel template

The 'angel' that the children are decorating is a representation of themselves, so once they know this, they will decorate the angel in a manner that links to their own dress sense, hair length and colour, and facial expressions.

Pose questions and collect class data

Once the angels have been decorated, ask children to bring 'themselves' to a clear space in the classroom (or gather around a large table). The table is clearly divided (by a piece of string or strip of paper) into two sections. The teacher presents two statements written on cards that are opposite to each other:

- people who have a pet/people who don't have a pet
- people who like chocolate ice cream the best/people who don't like chocolate ice cream the best

178   TEACHING EARLY YEARS MATHEMATICS, SCIENCE AND ICT

- people who had a piece of fruit at lunchtime/people who didn't have a piece of fruit at lunchtime
- people who would like to go on an excursion to the zoo/people who would like to go on an excursion to another place.

Children must decide on the category to which they belong and place themselves (their angel) into that category. A physical graph of the situation is the result. On first viewing, the category with the most children can be quickly determined. To find the actual number in each category, the data angels can be rearranged, either in groups (e.g. 2, 5) or in corresponding lines along the dividing line, so that quick calculations of the total can be determined. This activity can be extended to three choices, and hence a new graph/visual representation achieved. However, leaving it at two choices assists in helping children think of collecting data that requires a yes/no response.

Children collecting data through classroom routines

DATA ANGELS ROUTINE

The data angels activity can become a classroom routine by changing the categories on a daily basis. For example, before lunch break, all children ensure that their data angels are on their desks. After lunch, as a routine, the children collect their angels and move to the data table and decide the category to which they belong in this particular instance. The children come together at the data table and the teacher leads a discussion about the results of the survey.

To further extend this activity, in turn on a daily basis, each child is tasked with the responsibility of determining the two categories for the survey. The reasons they wanted to ask the question they posed are discussed, and hence the reason for collecting data is emphasised. The fact that the data angel is a representation, rather than a photo of each child, avoids a focus of attention on particular children. In most cases, children will be able to identify their own angel easily, but will not always remember who other angels belong to as they are displayed. This means that those who responded to particular survey items are not readily identified.

JUNIOR METEOROLOGISTS

Collecting daily weather data can become a class routine. This context provides opportunities to engage the children in various aspects of measurement and data collection. The task of being responsible for weather observations is assigned to different children every week. At the same time each day, the thermometer that is located on the wall outside the classroom is read and the temperature recorded. The teacher or other adult assists if the children have not yet been exposed to using measurement instruments or formal units of temperature. The child also selects one of the words to describe the weather—cloudy, sunny, windy and/or rainy—from a pile of cards. The children also check the rain gauge located outside the classroom and record any rainfall. These data are recorded and displayed on the classroom weather data display that is growing along the wall of the classroom. At various times in the term and school year, the teacher makes use of these data to build and extend mathematical knowledge. How many sunny days did we have in July? Which month had most sunny days? How much rain fell in February? Is this the wettest month? Are there any weeks in which we have had temperatures over 25 degrees Celcius? What patterns can you see in the data that we have collected?

> **Teaching point:** These activities provide a nice opportunity to use ICT. For example, weather apps or websites can be used to gather information about local weather. IWB programs can be used to display and discuss the information the children have gathered and digital weather stations are an effective way for the children to monitor the weather.

Conclusion

This chapter has focused on the teaching and learning of chance and data. As with the previous chapters, the ideas here have placed emphasis on helping children to make connections with what they know, what they have learned in other areas of mathematics and the world around them. Real-world examples are important for helping children to build a strong understanding of mathematical concepts and skills, and also an appreciation of the ways in which mathematics can be used in everyday life to solve problems and understand the world.

Planning and reflection

Use the Planning and Reflection for Teaching template in Chapter 1 to more deeply consider and make personal decisions about the pedagogy, curriculum and assessment possibilities or requirements for this unit.

Geometry and Measurement

This chapter provides ideas and teaching points about promoting young children's understanding of mathematical concepts associated with geometry (sometimes referred to as 'space') and measurement. While there are connections between topics in geometry and measurement, ideas for teaching topics in these strands are presented separately in this chapter. It is important that teachers remain vigilant for opportunities to develop concepts around geometry and measurement by taking advantage of the children's play environments or developing authentic contexts in the classroom.

Geometry

Developing mathematical knowledge about geometry for children in the early school years is about immersing them in structured play activities to promote awareness of their environment in a mathematical sense. For developing spatial understanding, the focus is on raising awareness of shapes and locations in the environment and providing the language to describe the three-dimensional (3D) world in two dimensions. Many of the activities in this section involve children creating and/or discussing products. This provides excellent assessment opportunities.

Focus 1: Two-dimensional (2D) shapes

Pattern blocks

Pattern blocks, shown in Figure 12.1, are a great resource to explore shapes and their properties. The blocks can be sorted according to colour, which also means sorting according to shape. Pattern blocks consist of triangles, squares, pentagons, hexagons, diamonds and trapezia. They can be used to build an understanding of:

- polygons—poly (many) gon (angle)—the name given to two-dimensional closed shapes with straight sides
- regular polygons—all have equal sides and equal angles
- naming shapes—for example, square, triangle, pentagon
- shapes that tessellate (no gaps or overlaps)—triangle, square, hexagon; combinations of shapes can make tessellating patterns
- fractions—two trapeziums make one hexagon; three triangles make one hexagon.

Figure 12.1   (a) Pattern blocks

Some activities using pattern blocks include:

- *Create patterns and designs*: make an extended repeating pattern, a radiating pattern that extends from a centre point or a spiral pattern.
- *Create a variety of 'creatures' from the shapes*: experiment with different colours or different shapes. Children can trace around each of the pattern blocks to show the template of the creature and the individual shapes from which it is made (examples can be seen in Figure 12.2).

Figure 12.2 Examples of shape activities

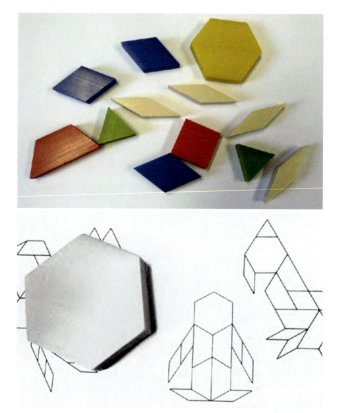

- *Use a large square template to find various combinations of shapes that can 'fill' the large square.*
- *Price a creature*: Assign differently shaped blocks particular values (e.g. square is 5c, triangle is 10c, hexagon is 20c, etc.). Calculate the cost of the creature. Create a creature of a particular value (e.g. $2.00).

Teaching point: In this activity, a clear link can be made to the Number and Algebra strand through the connection to money. These activities provide opportunities for teachers to assess children's understanding through instruments such as observation and checklisting.

Shape families
Due to repeatedly seeing representations of shapes in a particular orientation, some children believe that shapes can only be drawn or positioned in particular ways. For example, some children believe that all triangles must be represented as resting on their base, as in Figure 12.3. They believe that shapes in other orientations, such as the second orientation shown in Figure 12.3 are incorrect.

Figure 12.3 Identical triangles with different orientations

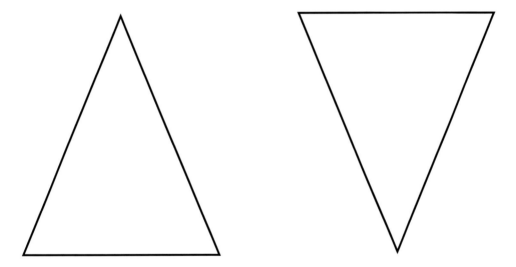

When children are learning about shapes and their properties, provide them with many examples to emphasise properties and to reduce the development of misconceptions about how shapes should be oriented on a page. The example in Figure 12.4 shows a family of shapes that share particular properties (i.e. they are all rectangles—shapes with both pairs of sides parallel and four 90 degree angles). There are three shapes that are the same (1, 2 and 4 are identical or congruent), yet research shows that children tend to identify only shapes 1 and 4 as the same.

Figure 12.4 A family of shapes in which 1, 2 and 4 are identical

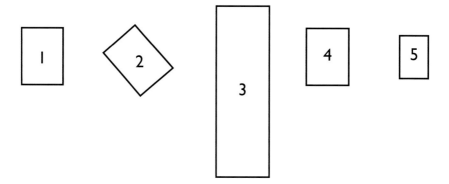

Coathanger art
The children can be provided with a range of 2D shapes on cards with a hole punched at a different point on each one. They can paint each shape and arrange them on a wire coathanger (with string) to create a mobile. Draw the children's attention to the different orientations of the shapes and question them about which are the same and which are different.

Making simple tessellations
Making tessellations can be an interesting extension activity to engage children with 2D shapes and patterning. Start with a square or a triangle, as these shapes both tessellate. Cut a section from the shape and slide it across the shape to the other side. Attach this new part of the shape to the original shape as shown in Figure 12.5.

Figure 12.5 Tessellating shapes

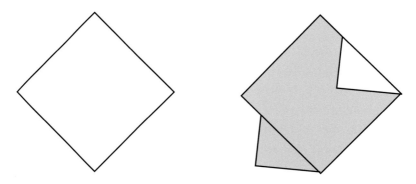

Through repeated cutting and sliding, new shapes can be created that will continue to tessellate, and can be used to make an interesting tessellating pattern. The process can be repeated to create more and more creative tessellating shapes. If the new shape becomes 'floppy' with the extra cuts and slides, the children can redraw the final shape on to new card and cut it out. They can then use this template to make a tessellating pattern and colour it in an interesting way for display. Children may need adult help with this activity.

> **Teaching point:** The children can use a range of digital drawing tools on the computer to create, colour and tessellate shapes. Their patterns can be printed and displayed in the classroom. They can also be added to the children's digital portfolios.

Flips, slides, turns

Exploring how shapes can flip, slide and turn involves learning about what shapes look like when they are reflected, translated and rotated. Cut out regular and irregular shapes from cardboard. The children can trace around them to explore how shapes can flip, slide and turn:

- *Flip (reflection)*: Draw a line (this is the reflection line) and place the shape with one edge on the line. Trace around the shape. Flip the shape across the line to create a mirror image of the shape. Trace around the shape again. Label this action as a flip on the paper.
- *Slide (translation)*: Draw a line and place the shape with one edge on the line. Trace around it. Now move the shape further along the line (keeping the edge on the line). Trace around the shape in its new position. Label this action as a slide on the paper.
- *Turn (rotation)*: Trace the shape. Holding the shape at one of its points (vertices), turn the shape using quarter-turns from that point, tracing the shape each time. Label these actions as turns on the paper.

> **Teaching point:** Completing this activity requires fine motor skills, so children may need assistance; however, it is also a good activity for allowing the children to practise using their fine motor skills. The children can make flips, slides and turns using drawing software on the computer or apps on a tablet. These translations can also be demonstrated using the IWB. As well as doing this activity with line sketches, the children can use pattern blocks and photograph the results. A further activity could involve the children themselves acting as the object that flips, slides or turns. Using such a variety

> of methods allows children to experience the same concepts using drawings, physical objects, kinaesthetic activities and digital representations. Digital representations can be placed on the IWB for class discussion.

Symmetry

Exploring symmetry is about noticing reflections of shapes or seeing how shapes can be divided equally in halves. Cut out pictures of regular and irregular shapes. Explore whether the shapes can be folded in half so that there are two equal halves of the same shape and size, which are reflections of one another. Draw the line of symmetry on those shapes and display. Note which regular shapes have lines of symmetry and whether they have more than one.

Focus 2: Three-dimensional (3D) shapes

Making 3D shapes

With a partner, the children can create regular 3D shapes such as a cube, a square-based pyramid and a tetrahedron with balls of plasticine or play dough and matchsticks (not matches) or short lengths of straws. A cube requires twelve matchsticks and eight balls of play dough. A square-based pyramid requires eight matchsticks and five balls of play dough. A tetrahedron requires six matchsticks and four balls of play dough. The resulting shapes clearly show the vertices (the play dough) and edges (the matchsticks) of each of these shapes, as shown in Figure 12.6. The children can share their shapes and then use this new terminology to describe their shapes to the class.

Place the shapes close to the edge of the desk. Ask children how they knew where the 'edge' of the desk was located. Link this to the 'edge'—the matchsticks—on each shape. Again, this allows the teacher to emphasise the precise language used when describing the features of these shapes.

> **Teaching point:** This activity can be duplicated using drawing or graphics software to be shared with the class on the IWB. The sharing and explaining provide good classroom practice in mathematics, as they provide children with opportunities to clarify their thoughts, use appropriate language and develop mathematical communication skills. The teacher could use a checklist while listening to the children's presentations to assess whether they have developed an understanding of the terminology.

Figure 12.6 Cube and tetrahedron made from play dough and matchsticks

Properties of shapes
Pose questions that require children to consider the shapes of various objects and to think about why particular shapes are the way they are:

- Why are ice-cream cones shaped the way they are?
- In what shape are most foods packaged? What types of foods are packaged in particular shapes that you know?
- What shape are the cells that bees make? Why do you think they create this shape?
- If we cut a hose into small pieces, what shapes will be created? (This activity can be done using play dough and a paddlepop stick as a cutting device.) The children can predict which 3D shapes will form and which 2D faces will be created.

The children can also photograph or draw, label and/or explain these or other shapes they observe around them. This provides further assessment opportunities.

188   TEACHING EARLY YEARS MATHEMATICS, SCIENCE AND ICT

Shape walk in the environment
Walk through the school grounds. Locate 2D and 3D shapes in the environment. Find tessellating patterns in the environment. Provide children with cameras so that they can take photos of various shapes and arrangements of shapes that they have located in their environment. Create a slide show of the photos to share in class.

Focus 3: Location and arrangement
Turn the classroom into a Pirate Island. Create murals and cut-outs of palm trees, sand and sea. Cover tables with sheets so that they became mountains. Use blue cellophane to make rivers that snake through the room. The children pretend that they are pirates landing on the island. They move around the island using directional and positional language: *cross* the river, go *under* the tree, go *through* the cave, go *around* the mountain, *turn left* at the boulder . . .

The children can draw a map of the classroom (or younger children can be given a template to label). This provides an opportunity for children to transform a 3D physical representation into a 2D diagrammatic representation. This requires children to consider relative size and location of objects. The teacher can guide this process using the IWB.

The map and the physical environment can now be used in a number of ways:

- Children can plan a route and treasure location using their map in 2D and then enact their route in the classroom. (The treasure could perhaps be a small coin or piece of costume jewellery.)
- They can do this in reverse by acting out the journey to the treasure and then plot their route on their map.
- They can provide a list of instructions to another group on how to get from the 'landing' place of the boat to the place of the buried treasure.
- The children can move through the island, following instructions such as: at the tree, skip three times; at the first mountain, crawl 1 metre; at the river, jump five times on the spot. They can create a second legend that communicates how they must move along the path: square means skip, cylinder means roll, oval means jump, diamond means crawl and star means walk.

Teaching point: The teacher can guide the children in using symbols to represent the landmarks in the room when drawing their maps. This introduces children to the idea of info-graphics, which involves the use of symbols or icons to represent objects or actions. Again, these activities and products provide the teacher with numerous assessment opportunities.

Measurement

In the first three years of school, measurement understanding draws upon children's experiences through play, such as in the sandpit or water activities. Children begin by making comparisons: which is longer or shorter, lightest or heaviest? By doing so, they develop the language of comparison. Later, they use informal units to make and order measures of attributes, such as length, area, mass, volume and capacity. For example, the ruler is three pencils long or the bucket holds six tins of sand. Sequencing events and noticing recurring events throughout the year promote children's understanding of time.

The ultimate purpose of measurement is to assign a numerical value to communicate the size or amount of something. In the early years of schooling, a valuable teaching sequence to develop measurement understanding is:

1. Identify the attribute (e.g. length, mass).
2. Compare and order.
3. Use non-standard units initially to compare and later to quantify.
4. Use standard units.

This sequence is useful as a reminder that there are many learning experiences that occur before children are expected to apply standard units of measure. The first step is to identify the attribute. In order to assign a measure to a particular 'thing', children need to be able to identify what that 'thing' actually is. When they come to school, they are very knowledgeable about tallness and height. They would have taken part in 'back-to-back' activities to determine whether they are taller than their friend, or whether they have grown. In doing such activities, children have already identified the attribute of tallness/height, and are comparing and ordering the measures. However, they would not generally consider that have been measuring their 'length'—yet exploring length is exactly what they have been doing.

> **Teaching point:** The four steps of the sequence have been presented here, but children are often not expected to deal with formal units in the early years of schooling. The first three steps of the sequence are the most important developmental steps in these years.

Focus 1: Activities for measurement concept development

Guided play activities

During play activities, children can be asked to identify attributes of length, mass, volume, capacity and area. The teacher's role is to draw attention to these attributes through questioning and explicit language:

190   TEACHING EARLY YEARS MATHEMATICS, SCIENCE AND ICT

- *Length*: Let's make a road for the truck with pencils. How many pencils long is the road? Is this truck as long as a pencil?
- *Area*: How many handprints does it take to cover this page? How many handprints to cover this bigger page? Which page has the bigger area? How do you know? How many of our handprint pictures can be spread out on the table? What about the bigger table? Which table has the bigger area (or surface)?
- *Mass:* Can you lift your little brother/sister/friend? Is your little brother heavier or lighter than you? Can you lift your teacher? Your teacher is much heavier than you, which means that the teacher has more mass than you. What about these two objects (e.g. truck and car)? Which one is heavier? Which one has the most mass? Place this series of objects in order from lightest to heaviest (by heft).
- *Volume:* What takes up the most space, the soccer ball or the tennis ball? What about the tissue box and the stapler? The one that takes up the most space has the greater volume. Order a series of classroom objects from least to greatest volume—this can be done by viewing and/or by feel.
- *Capacity:* Which cup holds the most sand? This cup has a greater capacity than the other one. What about the bucket? Of the two cups and the bucket, which has the greater capacity? This is a particularly good type of activity for ordering because children can check their response by filling the vessels with sand or water.

Consider carefully the objects that you use for helping children identify the attribute to be measured. If you provide children with a collection of balls for identifying the attribute of volume, they may focus on some other feature of the ball, such as colour or bounciness. The collection of objects you use to help children identify the attribute needs to be diverse and varied to ensure that the attribute is the focus and that children have an opportunity to describe that object in relation to that attribute.

> **Classroom example: Measurement in the sandpit:** In the sand pit, the teacher includes three cups, one that holds twice the quantity of the first, and another that holds four times the quantity of the first (and hence double the second—i.e. in the ratio 1:2:4).
>
> The teacher watches as the children use the cups to fill the tip truck but notices that the child with the smallest cup wants to swap with the child who is using the largest cup. The teacher joins the conversation and asks the children to state which cup is the smallest, largest, etc. The teacher then introduces the word 'capacity' by holding the

GEOMETRY AND MEASUREMENT   191

smallest cup and the largest cup and stating that the smaller cup holds less than the large cup, which means that the small cup has the least capacity of the two cups.

The children continue with the task of filling the truck, but the teacher draws attention to the word *capacity* by stating, 'Capacity, that's a funny word. What do you think it means? Capacity means the amount something can hold. The small cup holds less than the large cup. This cup (smallest cup) has the least capacity, but this cup (largest cup) has the greatest capacity.' The teacher repeats the words: least capacity, greatest capacity. The children repeat these words. They gesture to the small cup and then the largest cup stating 'least capacity, greatest capacity' respectively.

The teacher then asks how many small cups of sand are required to fill the middle cup, and how many middle cups of sand are required to fill the largest cup. The children work together, measuring, checking, counting and discussing their answers. The teacher asks how many small cups will be required to fill the biggest cup. The children guess and check. The teacher asks how they would be able to fill exactly half the middle cup.

Through teacher guiding and questioning, children are engaging with mathematics concepts associated with fractions, ratio and proportion. They are learning new language of capacity. The play-based learning experience has been made richer by the teacher's questions and the use of informal language being gradually replaced by formal mathematics language.

When the children are asked by the teacher to reflect on what they have done during the day, the teacher reminds the children of the new words that were learnt in the sandpit. With the three cups used in the sandpit on display, the teacher asks children to explain the difference between least capacity and greatest capacity. The children may not be able to define the term 'capacity' as the amount a container can hold, but they can compare and contrast the containers and use their new vocabulary of 'least capacity' and 'greatest capacity' in context.

The teacher invites other children into the conversation by asking them to think of other containers that may have greater capacity. The children identify the rubbish bin and state that its capacity is much greater than the large cup. They think about the tins that hold their pencils on their desks. They then think about their lunchboxes. The teacher asks them to experiment with measuring and comparing the capacity of other vessels at home.

Measuring and patterning

Comparing and ordering activities can link to patterning activities, and can reinforce the language associated with an attribute. A box of tall and short pencils can be used to create a repeating pattern (tall pencil, short pencil, tall pencil, short pencil—A B A B pattern). Children can use big squares and little squares to create a pattern, but also to describe the pattern in terms of a measurement attribute—small square

192 TEACHING EARLY YEARS MATHEMATICS, SCIENCE AND ICT

small area, big square big area, small square small area, big square big area. Cups can be lined up and described as having lesser capacity, greater capacity, lesser capacity, greater capacity and so on.

Through making comparisons, children will order various objects and use comparative language:

- long, longer, longest; short, shorter, shortest
- heavy, light, lighter; heavy, heavier, heaviest; light, lighter, lightest
- most mass, least mass
- greatest volume, least volume
- greatest capacity, least capacity.

> **Teaching point:** Check IWB software and tablet apps for further measuring and comparing activities. Bear in mind that attributes that relate to 2D figures work best with ICT. For example, it is easy to identify length or area. It is not easy for children to relate to attributes such as volume, capacity or mass in the same way. It is very important that children experience measurement attributes using physical objects before moving to virtual representations. Technologies do, however, allow children to deepen their understanding through experience with varied scenarios and new representations. They also provide new experiences with the representation of a 3D object in 2D. Using the reveal tool on the IWB can provide children with experiences with estimation.

Ideas for investigating length

Plasticine/play dough

- Make a long roll of plasticine/play dough.
- How many paperclips long is it?
- Roll a line of plasticine six paper clips long.

String (of various lengths)

- Find something as long as your string.
- Find something shorter, longer, taller than your string.

Circumference

- Cut lengths of string to measure around the middle of various cans.
- Glue each piece of string length on a piece of paper to make a graph showing the circumference/length around the middle of each can. Label each length of string according to the can it has measured.

GEOMETRY AND MEASUREMENT 193

I-spy
- Find things shorter/longer than the pencil.
- Find things that have greater/less area than the notice board.
- Find things that have greater/less capacity than the rubbish bin.

Ideas for investigating area
Geoboards
- Create a series of shapes to cover the geoboard.
- Can you cover the geoboard with only two shapes?
- Can you cover the geoboard with five different shapes that you know?

Square grid paper
- Draw shapes on the grid paper. Count the number of squares for each shape.
- Draw a square that is four grid squares in area. Draw a square that is one grid square in area.

Create quilts
- Use coloured squares and triangles (that are half the size of the square) to create a pattern that looks like a quilt—discuss why these shapes are good for quilts. This can be linked to the children's experiences with tessellations.
- Count how many squares and triangles were required for your quilt.
- If two triangles make one square, how many squares is your quilt?

Chocolate share pack
- Trace around the large packet in which the chocolates came.
- Estimate the number of individual chocolate wrappers that would be required to cover the area and compare this with the number of chocolates in the packet.
- Cover the area with chocolate wrappers.

Decorate your desk
- Use various uniform materials to cover the desk (e.g. squares of coloured paper, MAB 100s blocks; handprints; milk bottle tops). Relate the number of objects required to their size (e.g. there will be less handprints required than bottle tops because a hand has a greater area than a bottle top).

Ideas for investigating mass
Spin and weigh challenge
- Use a two-option spinner marked with *heavier* and *lighter*, a box of items and balance scales

194 TEACHING EARLY YEARS MATHEMATICS, SCIENCE AND ICT

- Select an item from the box, spin the spinner, find an item to match the instruction on the spinner, check on the balance scale which item is the heavier and which is the lighter.

Vegetable/fruit weighing

- Order a selection of fruit or vegetables (by heft) heaviest to lightest. Check with the balance scale.

> **Teaching point:** With all of these activities and ideas, look for opportunities to engage with ICT. Using the IWB allows for whole-class discussion, which in turn allows children to use the language associated with measurement and comparison. These kinds of activities should not be viewed as 'one-off' tasks. Children need regular opportunities to engage in such experiences and this type of thinking throughout the first three years of schooling. Teachers should use their imagination to vary the context, the objects used, the questions asked and the complexity of the task. In this way, they will continue to engage their children and to cater to their development.

Informal units to formal units

Using informal units is a means of communicating measures, provided that the units are of standard size. That is, if children are measuring the length of the whiteboard with their hand spans, there will be differences in the total measure due to differences in children's hand spans (assuming that there are no errors in measurement). However, if children use a standard measuring device, such as a particular pencil, they all should arrive at the same measurement of the length of the whiteboard in pencil lengths. When using informal units, it is important that units are standard so that accuracy in measurement is obtained.

> **Teaching point:** When children use informal non-standard units for measuring (such as hand spans for length, handfuls for capacity, handprints for area), they will often come to realise that they need to use standard units. If a decision is made to introduce children to formal units, an essential first step is to teach them how to read the measuring devices that are used for measuring with formal units. Children may be familiar with the language of formal units (centimetres and metres; grams and kilograms; litres and millilitres), but they need support in knowing the connections between these units and identifying the most appropriate unit for measuring particular objects or amounts.

GEOMETRY AND MEASUREMENT 195

Focus 2: More measurement ideas

Angle

The children can make an angle wheel by cutting out two circles from different-coloured paper, making a slit to the centre of each circle and joining the circles together. They can then explore the way different angles appear, showing a quarter-turn; half-turn and three-quarter turn. Connections can be made to the angles created using the angle wheel and the angles through which the children can turn with their bodies (i.e. stand and then turn on the spot so that you are now facing backwards—this is a half-turn).

Time

Learning about time involves learning about two aspects: measuring time (duration) and identifying a point in time (occurrence). Ideas for the teaching of time are presented in Chapter 13.

Problem-solving with measurement

Look for interesting opportunities for children to engage with measurement through problem-solving activities and extended investigations. Pose inquiry problems that require measurement:

- Find something that is approximately half of your height.
- Using play dough:
  - Make a small 'pizza base' and ask the children to make a pizza base that has twice the diameter of the first pizza base.
  - Pretend the play dough is bread dough; cut the bread dough into varying amounts of equal-sized bread rolls, depending on the children's readiness to deal with different numbers.
- Find two containers where the first container has exactly twice the capacity as the second.
- Create the best paper aeroplane. How do you know it is the best?
- Using two pieces of A4 paper create two cylinders. The first cylinder is created by rolling the paper widthways; the second cylinder is created by rolling the paper lengthways. Which cylinder holds the most or do they both hold the same? Fill each cylinder with separate unifix blocks to check.

Teaching point: Measurement relates well to many cross-curricular activities—for example, science and physical education. Look for real-world opportunities to create an imperative to learn about measurement.

Conclusion

In this chapter, we have presented ideas for developing children's understanding of geometry and measurement. There are many opportunities within and beyond the mathematics curriculum to introduce children to the concepts associated with these areas and to reinforce children's understanding. Whenever possible, teachers should identify authentic opportunities to engage children in geometry and measurement. For example, in science, children can be introduced to both formal units of time, temperature or length, as well as estimation and the use of comparative language. They can also begin to develop skills in drawing or labelling simple diagrams to represent 3D objects in 2D.

Planning and reflection

Use the Planning and Reflection for Teaching template in Chapter 1 to more deeply consider and make personal decisions about the pedagogy, curriculum and assessment possibilities or requirements for this unit.

Making ICT integral to mathematics: Time

In this chapter, we have deliberately placed a stronger emphasis on integrating ICT into the teaching and learning of the mathematics topic of time (part of the measurement strand) to highlight the powerful and exciting opportunities that ICT affords modern mathematics classrooms. We will indicate where possible, the ICT competencies of:

- investigating
- creating
- communicating
- managing and operating, and
- safe and ethical use.

Time is multi-faceted and developmental, so will be a topic that is regularly revisited. As with all aspects of the curriculum, it is up to teachers to make decisions regarding which concepts their children are ready to learn and the best ways in which to facilitate that learning. While time is an important element within the mathematics curriculum, it is also important in many other contexts and curricula—for example, topics that rely on the notion of sequencing; understanding timelines and relative lengths of time; or where an understanding of time durations is important. Because

198 TEACHING EARLY YEARS MATHEMATICS, SCIENCE AND ICT

of the developmental and cross-curricular nature of time-related concepts, this section uses foci rather than episodes to organise the different ideas presented.

Some of the ideas in this section can be adapted for use in a variety of ways. For example, creating a calendar or timeline can be done as a teacher-led class activity, or by children in pairs, groups or individually, depending on the learning goals and the children's readiness to work independently with the selected ICT. In addition, some activities presented as IWB activities could be adapted for use on tablets or computers and vice versa. The activities have been sequenced to move from larger units of time, such as those associated with the calendar—the months of the year, weeks and days—to smaller units of time, such as hours and minutes, which lead to telling the time.

FOCUS 1

The calendar

Exploring the months of the year

ICT COMPETENCE *Investigate with teacher guidance*

Many children come to school with an understanding that time is measured in days and months. For example, they may know the date or the month of their own or family members' birthdays. Many children will understand the concept of weekdays and weekends because their family routine differs on some days or changes at the weekend. Teachers of young children can build on these early understandings when introducing time by learning about the months and days using a calendar. On the IWB, the teacher can project a calendar, month by month. This can be used to explore the names and the order of the months of the year. Through class discussion, children can provide information about events that are significant to them or their families. Discussions such as these give the teacher an opportunity to gauge children's prior knowledge. They also provide opportunities to introduce children to the language of time.

> **ICT teaching point:** The IWB is a very useful tool to assist with teaching, and for enhancing the use of ICT within the classroom. IWBs can be used to promote discussion in the classroom. Kent (2008) suggested that they could be successfully used for sorting activities, ordering and sequencing activities, labelling activities, and puzzle simulation and game activities. These activity types all lend themselves to teaching and learning about time.

Creating a calendar

ICT COMPETENCE   *Create a teacher-generated product with children's participation*
ICT COMPETENCE   *Create a child-generated product with teacher guidance*

With the teacher's guidance, the class can build its own calendar using the IWB—there are many resources online (e.g. PowerPoint templates, apps) that can be used to create calendars by labelling significant events, using different colours to identify different days (e.g. to distinguish weekdays from weekends, school holidays from school days) or including pictures. Important school events can be added. Many children will have days that are culturally or personally significant to them (e.g. birthdays, Chinese New Year, Ramadan, Easter), which can also be added. If they are unsure of the dates, this is an opportunity for them to ask at home and collect some simple information about themselves. Including cultural events provides a nice way for children to learn about one another's backgrounds and cultures.

If they are ready, the children can create their own calendar—perhaps for the coming month—using computer programs or tablet apps. They can illustrate their calendar with seasonally appropriate images and use colours to show important school or family events or holidays. Calendars can be shared, used and added to children's digital portfolios.

Figure 13.1   Calendar created using a PowerPoint template

200   TEACHING EARLY YEARS MATHEMATICS, SCIENCE AND ICT

> **ICT teaching point:** Activities such as creating a class calendar allow the teacher to model a range of ICT skills for the children, which they can then practise when making their own calendars. Examples will vary depending on the ICT skills and writing levels of the children. They may include inserting pictures and clip art, creating textboxes, shading cells and formatting fonts.

Investigating the calendar: Months of the year

ICT COMPETENCE   *Create a child-generated product with teacher guidance*

The class calendar can be used to investigate various aspects of time, including sequencing (e.g. using the IWB to sequence months or seasons) and durations (e.g. the lengths of different months can be compared). A simple table, chart or graph could be created for the classroom to display the months of the year that have different numbers of days. This can be done as a class group or in smaller groups—perhaps pairs. Again, the range of software that can be used depends on the structure of the activity and availability of software, and the readiness of the children to work in small groups. The representations in Figure 13.2 were created using Inspiration, PowerPoint, and Word respectively.

Such illustrations provide an opportunity for discussion of which months have the most days or least days, or how February is different. If appropriate, the idea of a leap year can be linked to skip-counting in fours.

Investigating the calendar: Seasons

ICT COMPETENCE   *Investigate with teacher guidance through a range of sources*

Activities can be used with the IWB to allow children to link the months of the year to the different seasons, and to learn the order of the seasons. It may be interesting to discuss with the children the idea that children in other parts of the world are experiencing different seasons. For example, children in Australia may be fascinated to learn that children in Finland are experiencing weather very different from their own. The internet can be used to investigate the temperature in other countries. Other online resources, such as web cams, can also be useful for such investigations.

ICT COMPETENCE   *Create and communicate with child-generated products*

Children can create and share small presentations about each of the seasons and include pictures or clip art they find online to match what happens in each of the seasons. Presentations can be created using a variety of software—for example, Photo Story, PowerPoint, Word, or other age-appropriate software or apps.

MAKING ICT INTEGRAL TO MATHEMATICS: TIME   201

Figure 13.2   Different representations of the number of days in the month

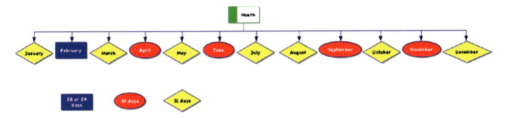

Months Of The Year

30 days
- September
- April
- June
- November

31 days
- January
- March
- May
- July
- August
- October
- December

28 days (except in leap years – 29 days)
- February

Number of days	Name of month
28 or 29	February
30	April June September November
31	January March May July August October December

Figure 13.3 A child presenting weather information using the IWB

These activities can be useful to make links to other curriculum areas—for example, science links can be made by discussing the ways in which seasonal changes influence behaviour or changes in nature (e.g. behaviour of animals, changes in plants, climatic variation).

> **ICT teaching point:** Ideas can be consolidated through the use of simulations or online games. For example, there are some fun online games and apps that children can play to make connections between seasons, climate, outdoor activities and weather-appropriate clothes.

Investigating the days of the week

ICT COMPETENCE   *Create child-generated product with or without assistance*

The days of the week can be included in the work on the calendar or they can become a separate focus. Learning about the days of the week provides an opportunity for further work with sequencing, and for counting and investigating number patterns using dates. Once again, the IWB is a great tool for sequencing the days of the week or matching aspects of school or family routines that take place on different days (e.g. sport on Fridays; music on Wednesdays; Italian language classes on Tuesdays and Thursdays; soccer practice on Thursdays). As with the calendar, children can create their own weekly planners, or this can be done as a class. If they create their own weekly planners, the children can include family events and other activities that are important to them.

The dates can be useful here for helping children to practise counting on and counting back. For example, it is Monday the 6th. What will the date be in three days' time? What was the date two days ago? How many days is it until the 10th? How many days ago was it the 1st? What is the date next Monday? How many days is it since . . . ? The IWB can be used as a tool to allow the children to check their answers.

Investigating daily routines

ICT COMPETENCE   *Create a child-generated product*
ICT COMPETENCE   *Communicate and share with others*

School and family routines can be useful for introducing the idea of sequencing, especially for younger children. For example, children can use the IWB to sequence and discuss activities that occur on a daily basis—for example, breakfast, go to school, morning session, recess, middle session, lunch (eating time, play time), afternoon session, go home, dinner, bath, bed. These can also be useful as a way of introducing children to the idea of times of the day—for example, morning, noon, afternoon, evening, night and finally to specific times. Blank timelines that the children can complete with their own information are available online. Children could search online for some time-lapse video clips showing changes that occur throughout the day. They can make their own sequences by setting up a camera on a tripod and recording images at regular time intervals during the school day (some digital cameras can be programmed to do this and thus could record photos in the hours beyond the school day).

Children enjoy playing with their pets or a favourite toy. Another way to focus on sequencing is to have the children record digital images and create a storyboard of their toy engaged in different daily tasks, such as eating breakfast, getting ready for school, playing at lunchtime, brushing their teeth and going to bed. A sample sequence is shown in Figure 13.4. As with many activities associated with time, this activity can be extended into other curriculum areas. For example, to merge into a literacy activity, the children can convert their storyboards into cartoons (using online cartoon-makers), a story that is presented orally—perhaps to classmates or to another class—or a storybook.

A variation of this involves children using a class figure—for example, a Lego man. The children can take the figure home and each child can record daily photos of a different routine. The children's collective photos can be used to create a class storybook to which all children have made a contribution.

Figure 13.4 Charles in the morning—a time sequence of activities for a child's toy

7:00 am
Charles wakes up

7:15 am
Charles eats breakfast

7:30 am
Charles brushes his teeth

7:45 am
Charles gets ready for school

FOCUS 2

Time

A number of different aspects of time can be covered with children in the first years of school. These include time-telling (initially to half and quarter hours); learning to tell the time with analogue and digital clocks; estimating lengths of time (becoming familiar with lengths of time); learning the relationships between months, weeks, days and hours; and sequencing and comparing events based on duration. Activities and investigations related to time can also provide useful data that children can represent using a variety of ICT. Learning to tell the time with an analogue clock also provides opportunities for learning about the concepts of 'clockwise' and 'anti-clockwise'.

Telling the time

ICT COMPETENCE *Creating a teacher-generated instructional tool*

Children can begin to tell the time by focusing on the hour, then the half hour, and then quarter and three-quarter hours. This, of course, requires links to be made to other work relating to fractions. It is important that children learn to tell the time using both analogue and digital clocks. Understanding how each hand on an analogue clock represents certain aspects of time (i.e. minutes, hours) is crucial when learning to tell the time. The IWB can be a useful tool for teachers to develop children's understanding of the way a clock functions and to introduce time-telling. Tablet devices have great apps for children to complete similar exercises independently or in small groups. The images in Figure 13.5 show screenshots from an IWB clock face that allows the minute hand to be moved while the hour hand moves accordingly.

Figure 13.5   A series of IWB clock images (created using <www.teacherled.com/resources/clockspin/clockspinload.html>

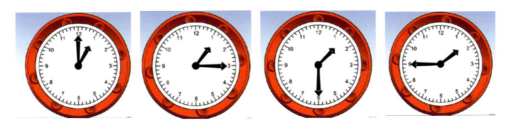

ICT COMPETENCE   *Creating a child-generated product; Teacher generated instructional resources*

There are many digital resources that can assist children to learn to tell the time—for example, interactive online games that require children to match analogue clocks to the digital time. These games can be played 'against the clock' or against another child. PowerPoint and other software and apps allow children to create their own clocks to show particular times. These are also useful for teachers to create IWB activities for use with children.

> **ICT teaching point:** Apps can help children to develop their skill level in literacy, numeracy and science, as well as other curriculum areas. Generally the apps have engaging graphics and a wide variety of activities available for the children. It is important to choose apps wisely to assist children with their development. Many education authorities and departments have lists of recommendations available.

Learning games can be used for drill and practice, or to promote problem-solving skills. When learning about time, children can use some games to simply improve the speed and accuracy of their time-telling ability. Other games will offer children more challenging time-related problems that require them to apply what they have learnt to new situations.

There are many ways to engage children in discussions about routines and activities that occur at particular times. For example, matching activities such as the one shown in Figure 13.6 can be used on the IWB or a tablet to help children link times to familiar activities.

206   TEACHING EARLY YEARS MATHEMATICS, SCIENCE AND ICT

Figure 13.6   Matching activity for linking time with daily school activities

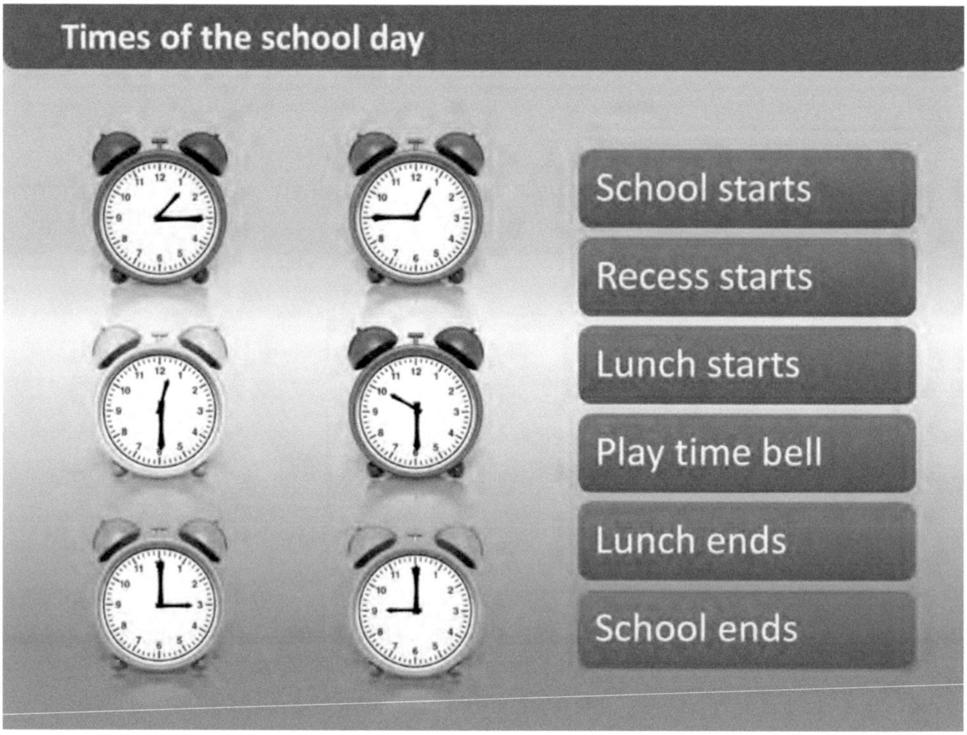

Investigating lengths of time

Children do not always have a sense of how long particular time intervals can be or their relative lengths. The ways in which they can engage in learning about durations of time are limited only by teachers' imaginations. Here are some simple ideas:

- Children can count how many times they can clap in fifteen seconds as they watch a timer, stop-watch, or clock with a second hand (either hand-held or on the IWB). This can be repeated for other activities such as stomping their foot, blinking or hopping. The results can be compared for different activities; data can be gathered and represented in numerous ways using ICT.
- Once the children have counted the number of times they can do something in fifteen seconds, they can make some predictions about other durations of time—for example, by asking them, 'How many times do you think you could clap in 30 seconds? One minute?'
- These activities can also be introduced by asking the children to estimate or predict before they start. They can be extended by using outdoor activities, such as running between cones, by varying the distance between cones or by changing the duration of time.

Other activities that focus on time

Literature and movies

ICT COMPETENCE   *Creating child-generated products*
ICT COMPETENCE   *Communicating and sharing products*

Stories often have reference to time, and many stories do have events that occur in order or in a time sequence. These can be used to develop or discuss certain vocabulary—for example, 'once upon a time'; 'happily ever after'; then, before or after. The main events in the story can be placed on cards or in text boxes, and children can be asked to arrange them according to their chronological order. Children can use a range of digital tools to create their own story or picture book that involves time sequences. Using a strategy similar to that mentioned for daily sequences (as illustrated in Figure 13.4), the children can use a favourite toy or character (such as a teddy bear) to create their time sequence stories by photographing their main character, downloading the images on to slides and then adding story text (with assistance if needed). This can also be done using cartooning software. Children can present their stories to their classmates or to another class.

Relative times

ICT COMPETENCE   *Investigate using digital resources*

Discussing events that occur weekly, monthly or yearly can help to develop children's understanding of relative lengths of time. For example, most children know that they have to wait a long time between birthdays, but that weekends come around much more often. They can use their calendars to count how many days, weeks or months between, since or until events. Seeing these relative times on a yearly calendar on the IWB will assist in developing these relative concepts.

Collecting data

ICT COMPETENCE   *Investigate and collect digital data*
ICT COMPETENCE   *Manage data—file and sort*
ICT COMPETENCE   *Create graphical representations; time-lapse sequences*

Collecting data about *how long* and *how many* can provide opportunities to collate and present data. For example, children can collect data when they count the number of claps in fifteen seconds and then use appropriate software to create tables and graphs that show how many children clapped a particular number of times. Time-lapse activities such as recording digital photographs of a shadow each hour of the day and creating a photo sequence can help children to understand the passing of time and the fact that some changes around them can be so slow that they aren't easily noticed.

Data collected in other subjects, such as science, often have a time element. For example, if children are investigating life-cycles or growth in science, they can photograph the animal or plant that is involved to create a digital photo sequence that illustrates change over time.

Conclusion

Throughout this chapter, we have focused on the use of ICT to support the teaching and learning of concepts associated with time. There are many opportunities for assessing both children's understanding of the mathematical concepts involved and their development of a range of ICT competencies. This chapter illustrates the idea that curriculum areas can be integrated and children can be exposed to concepts from one area through activities that have another focus. For example, in literacy activities when children discuss stories they have read or viewed, or when they create their own stories, there is often an opportunity for the teacher to focus on time concepts, including duration and sequencing. If the children use ICT to create their stories then of course there are also ICT teaching and assessment opportunities.

Planning and reflection

Use the Planning and Reflection for Teaching template in Chapter 1 to more deeply consider and make personal decisions about the pedagogy, curriculum and assessment possibilities or requirements for this unit.

A final note

Teaching children in the first three years of schooling is a challenging and rewarding career. It is vital that children in these years are given the opportunity to love learning, a disposition that will be the foundation of the lifelong learning to come. In this book, we have given insights into ways of approaching the teaching of science and mathematics with a particular focus on ICT integration that will contribute to positive teaching and learning experiences. As teaching in these years needs to be responsive to the young learner, it is important that the ideas in this text are seen as practical examples that could be shaped to your particular cohort and circumstances.

While we have presented the ideas in this book along curriculum lines (i.e. science, mathematics and ICT), it is not our intention that these curriculum areas should be taught in isolation. Effective instruction in the early years of schooling requires the teacher to make as many connections as possible between children's out-of-school and in-school experiences, as well as connections among and across different learning areas. It is up to teachers to use and adapt the ideas in ways that are most appropriate for their contexts and the children in their care.

We hope that all users of this book will find it a valuable source of ideas to enrich the experiences of teachers and children in the first three years of schooling.

References

Australian Curriculum, Assessment and Reporting Authority (ACARA). (2013). *Draft Australian Curriculum: Technologies*. Canberra: Australian Government.

Ausubel, D. P. (1968). *Educational psychology: A cognitive view*. New York: Halt, Rinehart and Winston.

Ben-Zeev, T. and Star, J. (2008). Intuitive mathematics: Theoretical and educational implications. In B. Torff and R. J. Sternberg (Eds.), *Understanding and teaching the intuitive mind* (pp. 29–56). Mahwah, NJ: Erlbaum.

Board of Studies. (1997). *Mathematics: Exemplary assessment tasks for Years P-2*. Carlton, Australia: Board of Studies.

Buckingham, D. (2005). *Media education: Literacy, learning and contemporary culture*. Malden, MA: Polity Press.

Bybee, R. and McCrae, B. (2011). Scientific literacy and student attitudes: Perspectives from PISA 2006 science. *International Journal of Science Education, 33*(1), 7–26.

Campbell, A. and Scotellaro, G. (2009). Learning with technology for pre-service early childhood teachers. *Australasian Journal of Early Childhood, 34*(2), 11–18.

Campbell, C. and Jobling, W. (Eds.). (2012). *Science in early childhood*. London: Cambridge University Press.

Carpenter, T. P. and Lehrer, R. (1999). Teaching and learning mathematics with understanding. In E. Fennema and T. A. Romberg (Eds.), *Mathematics classrooms that promote understanding* (pp. 19–32). Mahwah, NJ: Erlbaum.

Copley, J. (2006). *The young child and mathematics*. Washington, DC: National Association for the Education of Young Children (NAEYC).

Department of Education and Early Childhood Development. (2013). *Early Numeracy Research Project*. Retrieved from http://www.education.vic.gov.au/school/teachers/teachingresources/discipline/maths/pages/enrp.aspx

Department of Education and Training, Victoria. (2003). *Questioning categories: A report prepared by Deakin University.* Melbourne, Australia: State of Victoria.

Department of Education, Employment and Workplace Relations (DEEWR). (2010). *Educators belonging, being and becoming: Educators guide to the Early Years Learning Framework for Australia.* Produced by the Australian Government Department of Education, Employment and Workplace Relations for the Council of Australian Governments.

Department of Education, Employment and Workplace Relations (DEEWR). (2009). *Belonging, being and becoming: The Early Years Learning Framework for Australia.* Produced by the Australian Government Department of Education, Employment and Workplace Relations for the Council of Australian Governments.

Education Queensland. (1998). *Year 2 diagnostic net.* Brisbane: Queensland Government. Retrieved from http://education.qld.gov.au/students/policy/assessment/y2dn

Eshach, H. and Fried, M. N. (2005). Should science be taught in early childhood? *Journal of Science Education and Technology, 14*(3), 315–336.

Fleer, M. (2009). Understanding the dialectical relations between everyday concepts and scientific concepts within play-based programs. *Research in Science Education, 39*(2), 281–306.

Frank, A. R. (1989). Counting skills–a foundation for early mathematics. *The Arithmetic Teacher, 37*(1), 14–17.

French, L. (2004). Science as the centre of a coherent, integrated early childhood curriculum. *Early Childhood Research Quarterly, 19*, 138–149.

Gardner, H. (1999). *The disciplined mind: What all students should understand.* New York: Simon & Schuster.

Gialamas, V. and Nikolopoulou, K. (2010). In-service and pre-service early childhood teachers' views and intentions about ICT use in early childhood settings: A comparative study. *Computers & Education, 55*, 333–341.

Hennessy, S., Deaney, R. and Ruthven, K. (2005). *Emerging teacher strategies for supporting subject teaching and learning with ICT.* 1–14.

Hilton, G. (2007). Students representing mathematical knowledge through digital filmmaking. In J. Watson & K. Berwick (Eds.), *30th Annual Conference of the Mathematics Education Research Group of Australasia: Mathematics: Essential research, essential practice* (Vol. 1, pp. 382–391). Hobart, Australia: MERGA Inc.

Hilton, A., and Hilton, G. (2013). Incorporating digital technologies into science classes: Two case studies from the field. *International Journal of Pedagogies and Learning, 8*(3), 153–168.

Hobbs, R. (2006). Multiple visions of multimedia literacy: Emerging areas of synthesis. In M. C. McKenna, L. D. Labbo, R. D. Kieffer and D. Reinking (Eds.), *International handbook of literacy and technology.* (Vol. 2, pp. 15–28). Mahwah, NJ: Lawrence Erlbaum Associates.

Kent, P. (2008). *Interactive whiteboards: A practical guide for primary teachers.* Sydney, Australia: Macmillan Education.

Kimber, K. and Wyatt-Smith, C. (2006). Using and creating knowledge with new technologies: a case for students-as-designers. *Learning, Media and Technology, 31*(3), 19–34.

Koehler, M. J. and Mishra, P. (2005). What happens when teachers design educational technology? The development of technological pedagogical content knowledge. *Journal of Educational Computing Research, 32*(2), 131–152.

Lee, L. and O'Rourke, M. (2006). Information and communication technologies: transforming views of literacies in early childhood settings. *Early Years, 26*(1), 49–62.

Mackenzie, J, (1997). A questioning toolkit. *From Now On: The Educational Technology Journal, 7*(3). Retrieved from http://fno.org/nov97/toolkit.html

Metiri Group. (2006). *Technology in schools: What the research says.* Culver City, CA: Cisco Systems.

Mishra, P. and Koehler, M. J. (2006). Technological pedagogical content knowledge: A framework for teacher knowledge. *Teachers College Record, 108*(6), 1017–1054.

Organisation for Economic Cooperation and Development (OECD). (2012). *Starting strong III: A quality toolbox for early childhood education and care, OECD Publishing.* Retrieved from http://dx.doi.org/10.1787/9789264123564-en

Prain, V. (2006). Learning from writing in secondary science: Some theoretical and practical implications. *International Journal of Science Education, 28*(2–3), 179–201.

Prain, V. and Waldrip, B. (2010). Representing science literacies: An introduction. *Research in Science Education, 40*, 1–3.

Queensland Government. (2006). *Early years curriculum guidelines.* Spring Hill, Brisbane: Queensland Studies Authority.

Raffini, J. P. (1993). *Winners without losers: Structures and strategies for increasing student motivation to learn.* Upper Saddle River, NJ: Prentice Hall.

Ramadas, J. (2009). Visual and spatial modes in science learning. *International Journal of Science Education, 31*(3), 301–318.

Roblyer, M. D. and Doering, A. H. (2013). *Integrating educational technology into teaching.* Boston: Pearson.

Sheridan, S. and Pramling Samuelsson, I. (2003). Learning through ICT in Swedish early childhood education from a pedagogical perspective of quality. *Childhood Education, 79*(5), 276–282.

Siry, C., Ziegler, G. and Max, C. (2012). 'Doing Science' through discourse-in-interaction: Young children's science investigations at early childhood level. *Science Education, 96*(2), 311–336.

Skamp, K. (2008). *Teaching primary science constructively* (3rd ed.). South Melbourne, Australia: Cengage Learning.

Thompson, S., Rowe, K., Underwood, C. and Peck R. (2005). *Numeracy in the early years: Project Good Start.* Final report to the Australian Government Department of Education, Science and Training. Melbourne, Australia: ACER.

Thwaite, A. and McKay, G. (2013). Five-year-olds doing science and technology: How teachers shape the conversation. *Australian Journal of Language and Literacy, 36* (1), 28–37.

Van Oers, B. (2010). Emergent mathematical thinking in the context of play. *Educational Studies in Mathematics, 74* (1), 23–37.

Watters, J. J. and Ginns, I. S. (2000). Developing motivations to teach elementary science: effect of collaboration and authentic learning. *Journal of Science Teacher Education, 11*(4), 301–321.

Wolpert, L. (1993). *The Unnatural Nature of Science.* London: Faber & Faber.

Zevenbergen, R. and Logan, H. (2008). Computer use by preschool children: Rethinking practice as digital natives come to school. *Australasian Journal of Early Childhood, 33*(1), 37–44.

Zimmerman, C. (2000). The development of scientific reasoning skills. *Developmental Review, 20*, 99–149.

Index

active learner skills 140
addition 154
  basic facts, learning 164–5
    associative law 165
    commutative law 165
    fact families 169
    121 addition facts 166, 169
  growth points 165
  number families 169
  problem types, presentation of 155
  strategies approach 165
    bridging ten 168
    counting-on 166–7
    doubles and adding 10 167
    near doubles 169
    tens facts 167
algebra
  number patterns 161–3
    function machines 163–4
    99 board 161–2
    rainbow numbers 163
    skip counting 161
  patterning 160–1
    IWB, use of 160

    two-element repeats 160
angles
  concept development activities 195
animal homes unit 32–42
  animals losing their homes 37–9
    class discussion 37
    loss of habitat 38
    role-play activity 39
    viewing activity 39
  do animals have homes 33–7
    class discussion 33, 35
    classification activity 36
    field trip 37
    KWHL chart 35
    matching activity 35
    viewing activity 35
  making animal homes activity 40
  objectives 32
  overview of topic 32
  science skills *see* science skills
  science understanding 32
  topic extension, ideas 41–2
    communal homes 42
    mutual benefit arrangements 41

216 TEACHING EARLY YEARS MATHEMATICS, SCIENCE AND ICT

animal homes unit (*continued*)
  what is a home 32–3
    activity 33
    class discussion 32–3
annotations 4–5
apps, use and selection of 205
area
  concept development activities 189, 193
asking questions
  developing the skill of 33, 99
assessment
  ICT skills 20–1
  learning, of 3
  mathematics–
    class-room based 136–7
    external 137
    learning experiences, alignment with 137
  methods 4–7
  self-assessment 6
  specific tasks 5
Ausubel 2

Beaufort Scale 81
biological science 26
  animal homes *see* animal homes unit
  colour in nature *see* colour in nature unit
  geometry and measurement, integration of 31
  ICT, integration into 31–2
  mathematics, integration into 31–2
  nature of 31
  number and algebra, integration of 31
  science skills *see* science skills
bubbles unit
  bubbles in everyday life 67
  guided play 61
  inside a bubble activity 62–4
  making bubbles 62
  nature of 61
  science understanding 61
  topic extension ideas 67

calendar 198–204
  creating 199
  daily routines, investigating 203–4
  days of the week 202–4
  months, exploration of 198–9
  representations of data 201
  seasons 200, 202
capacity
  concept development activities 189
    sandpit 191
chance concepts 173
  certain and impossible events 174
  two-outcome spinner 174
checklists 5
chemical science 26, 52
  bubbles *see* bubbles unit
  ICT, integration into 53
    digital cameras 53
    IWB 53
  mathematics, integration of 53
    geometry and measurement 31
    number and algebra 53
    statistics and probability 53
  mixing *see* mixing unit
  nature of 52
  skills *see* science skills
children
  curiosity of 25
  pre-school mathematical knowledge 124–5
  prior understandings 2
classification, skill of
  classify and explain 93
  collecting data and 98
  play-based maths learning 128
  using reason to 35–6, 83, 92
classroom discourse, learning through 129–31
clock images, IWB 205
collaborative work
  ICT, while using 11
collisions study unit
  crashing to earth 99–102

demonstration activity 101
  stimulus image, use of 100
  tabulating of data 101
nature of science 99
overview of topic 99
protection from injury 108–9
  construction activity 108–9
science understanding 99
scratch and dent hunt 106–8
  collection of data 106
  discussion of observations 107–8
slow motion wrecks 102–6
  collecting data digitally 102–6
topic extension ideas 109
colour in nature unit
  drawing and labelling 49
  lost and found, visual activity 45–8
  nature of science 43
  overview of topic 43
  painting activity 47
  science understanding 43
  topic extension ideas 50–1
  where is it? activity 43–5
colours, mixing 56–8
  digital technologies, use of 58
  paint chart, creating 56
computer sharing 13
  laboratories 13
  mini labs 13
  mobile ICT 13
concept maps 117–18, 120
  Kidspiration 118
  software and apps 118
contexts for learning 127, 131
counting 140–6
  extending 143–6
  growth points in 141
  representations of numbers 141–3
  skip counting 143
    100s and 1000s, in 145–6
    tens, in 144–5
    twos, in 145

stages –
  point 141
  rational 141
  rote 140
subitising 143

daily routines
  daily weather data 179–9
  data collection activity and 178
  maths learning and 135
  time concepts and 203–4
data
  collection activities 176
    purposes of 176
  data angel activity 177–8
    daily routine, as part of 178
  diagrams, use of 33
  forms of representation 73
  gathering, activities 44, 72–3, 88
  symbols, use of 93
  tables and graphs, use of 44, 72–3, 101
  weather data 178–9
diagrams, use of 33
digital cameras 21, 31
  collecting data using 102–6, 116
  importance of 116
  integration into–
    biological science 31
    chemical science 53
  manipulation, ethics of 116
  record and represent information, to 37
  recording data activities 74
  safe and ethical use of 116
  uses of 116
  video technology–
    production 23, 83, 96, 117
    watching 10, 16, 53, 55, 117
'digital divide' 12
digital microscopes 79
digital portfolios 6
division 158, 160
  partition 158
  quotition 160

218   TEACHING EARLY YEARS MATHEMATICS, SCIENCE AND ICT

documentaries
  teacher pre-viewing of 39

The Early Years Numeracy Project 137
  numeracy 'growth points' 137, 165
    addition, in 165
    counting, in 141
earth and space science 26, 70
  ICT, integration of 72
  mathematics, integration of–
    geometry and measurement 70
    number and algebra 70
    statistics and probability 71
  nature of 70
  puddles and ponds *see* puddles and
    ponds unit
  skills *see* science skills
  wind *see* wind study unit
Educators Belonging, Being and Becoming:
  Educators' Guide to the Early
  Framework for
Australia 131

field trips
  'hunting and collecting' instinct 37
  recording data activities 74
  science skills, development of–
    biological science 37, 48, 120
    chemical science 60
    earth and space science 74, 78
    physical science 106
fractions 146–50
  doubling 147
    visualisation activity 147
  halving 146
    mental computation, as 149
  number line 147–9
    fractions on the empty 150
function machines 163–4

Gauss 163
geometry
  concepts 180

integration into–
  biological science 31
  chemical science 53
  earth and space science 70
  physical science 90
location and arrangement activity 188
shape walk 188
three-dimensional shapes
  making 186
  properties of 187
two-dimensional shapes 181
  coathanger mobiles activity 184
  flips (reflection) 185
  pattern blocks , activities 182
  shape families 183
  slides (translation) 185
  symmetry 186
  tessellating shapes 184–5
  turns (rotations) 185
group work
  ICT, while using 11
grouping and regrouping tasks 151–3
  multiplication activities 155
guided discovery 2

ICT
  animations, use of 21–2
  assessment of skills 20–1
  biological science, integration into 31–2,
    110–22
    offspring *see* offspring study unit
  checklists 5
  chemical science, integration into 53
  choice of, criteria 18–19
  currency of practice 24
  'digital divide' 12
  earth and space science, integration into
    72
  future development 24
  hardware, choice of 18–19
  infrastructure 13
  integration of 16–17
  learner response systems 23–4

learning benefits of 11
learning objectives and 20
new learning opportunities 21
non-linear nature of 15–16
physical science, integration into 91
play, role of 10–11
pre-school interaction 9
prevalence and importance of 10
resources, teacher-generated 17–18
robotics 22–3
simulations 21–2
software, choice of 18–19
teacher challenges 12
teacher learning with 21
TPACK, use of 15
types of resources 20
what constitutes 10
ICT resources
  drill and practice 20
  instructional games 20
  problem-solving 20
  teacher-generated 20
info-graphics 188
inquiry learning 2
interactive books 112
interactive whiteboard (IWB) 11, 15, 17–18
  books, use of online 112
  integration into–
    biological science 31, 35, 112
    chemical science 53
  measurement software 194
  patterns, for creation of 160
  pedagogical adaptations of 15
  time concepts, use in 198
    clock images 205
  word wall/wordle and 44, 112–13
internet
  guided use of 122
  safe, ethical use of 10, 12, 16, 18, 21, 112, 120
  YouTube 120
interviews 6

Kidspiration 118
kitchen gardens 3, 131
  growing plants activity 132–4
    monitoring growth 133
    planting 132
    watering 134
  who lives in the garden 131–2
    maths problem solving task 132
  worm farm activities 134–5
KWHL chart 35

learner
  prior understandings 2
learner response systems 23–4
learning
  assessment 4
  diversity of experiences 3
  play-based 2, 61
length
  concept development activities 189, 192–3
listening, respectful 3

Mackenzie, Jamie 4
manipulation
  cameras and ethics of 116
  context 45
  materials 72, 84–6, 108
maps
  location and arrangement activity 188
mass
  concept development activities 189, 193–4
mathematics
  addition *see* addition
  algebra *see* algebra
  assessing learning
    classroom based 136–7
    external 137
    learning experiences, alignment with 137
  biological science, integration into –
    geometry and measurement 31

mathematics (*continued*)
biological science, integration into – (*continued*)
number and algebra 31
statistics and probability 31
checklists 5
chemical science, integration into –
geometry and measurement 53
number and algebra 53
statistics and probability 53
class discourse, learning through 129–31
contexts for learning 127, 131
daily routines and learning 135
geometry *see* geometry
kitchen garden *see* kitchen gardens
measurement *see* measurement
multiplication *see* multiplication
numbers *see* numbers
play-based learning 2, 125–9
range of resources 126
teacher extending and encouraging 126
pre-school knowledge 124–5
robotics, use of 22–3
subtraction *see* subtraction
teaching styles–
connectionist 125
discovery 125
transmission 125
The Early Years Numeracy Project 137
measurement
concept development activities 189
angles 195
area 190
capacity 190
length 190, 192–3
mass 190
volume 190
informal to formal units 194
IWB software 192
integration into–
biological science 31
chemical science 53, 59

patterning and 191–2
play-based learning
sand pit 126, 190–1
shapes 127
problem-solving with 195
purpose of 189
teaching sequence 189
time *see* time
mixing unit
colours, mixing 56–8
digital technologies, use of 58
paint chart, creating 56
ice cream, making 58–61
experiment 58–9
measurement, integration of 59
unusual mix demonstration 54–5
money mathematics 153–4
activities 153
money clumps 154
movement study unit
exploring the ways things move 96–7
collecting/classifying forms of transport 98
obstacle course 97
how we make things move 92–5
push and pull 92–5
nature of science 91
overview of topic 91
science understanding 91
topic extension ideas 97
what is movement 91–2
classify and observe 92
role-play 91–2
wordle chart for movement words 96
multiplication 155–8
arrays 156–7, 159
basic facts, learning 164–5
associative law 165
commutative law 165
cross-product 155–6
grouping 155
growth points 165
proportional reasoning 154–6

rate problems 155–6
strategies approach 165, 170–1
  easy facts 170–1
  number grid 171

non-written presentations 6
number line 147–9
  fractions on the empty 150
number patterns 161–3
  99 board 161–2
  rainbow numbers 163
  skip counting 161
numbers
  addition *see* addition
  counting 140–6
    extending 143–6
    growth points in 141
    point 141
    rational 141
    representations, multiple 141–3
    rote 140
    stages 140–1
    subitising 143
  division 158, 160
    partition 158
    quotition 160
  fractions 146–50
    halving and doubling 146–7, 149
    number line 147–50
  integration into–
    biological science 31
    chemical science 53
    earth and space science 70
    physical science 90
  money mathematics 153–4
    activities 153
    money clumps 154
  multiplication 155–8
    arrays 156–7, 159
    cross-product 155–6
    grouping 155
    proportional reasoning 154–6
    rate problems 155–6

number families 169–70
number line 147–9
number patterns 161–3
  99 board 161–2
  rainbow numbers 163
  skip counting 161
organisation of objects 139
patterning 139
place value 150–3
  chicken scramble 151–2
  grouping and regrouping tasks 151–3
  packaging Cubi-jubes 152–3
pre-school knowledge 139–40
skip counting 143
  100s and 1000s, in 145–6
  tens, in 144–5
  twos, in 145
subtraction
  basic facts of 169–70
types of numbers–
  cardinal 146
  nominal 146
  ordinal 146

offspring study unit
  case study of self 114–18
    concept mapping 117–18
    data collection and representation
      114–15
    photo gallery 115–16
  nature of science 110
  overview of the topic 111
  science understanding 110
  topic extension ideas 120–1
  vocabulary development 112
  watching offspring grow 119
    VoiceThread 119
    wikis 119
  young plants and animals 111–14
    interactive books 112
    matching activity 114
organisation of objects 139

222 TEACHING EARLY YEARS MATHEMATICS, SCIENCE AND ICT

partition 158
patterning 124, 139, 160–1
  function machines 163–4
  IWB, use of 160
  number patterns 161–3
    99 board 161–2
    rainbow numbers 163
    skip counting 161
  two-element repeats 160
pedagogies, knowledge of 15
permanent/temporary concept 76–7
physical science 26, 90
  collisions *see* collisions study unit
  ICT, integration into 91
  mathematics, integration into–
    geometry and measurement 90
    number and algebra 90
    statistics and probability 91
  movement *see* movement study unit
  nature of 90
place value 150–3
  chicken scramble 151–2
  grouping and regrouping tasks 151–3
  packaging Cubi-jubes 152–3
play-based learning 2
  mathematics 125–9
    classifying 129
    contexts for 128
    sand pit (measurement) 126, 190–1
    shops 128
    traffic signs (shapes) 126–7
portfolios 6
  assessment, used for 137
  digital 6
  mobile phone access to 18
problem-solving
  stages of 5
proportional reasoning 154–6
puddles and ponds unit
  making puddles activity 72
    data gathering 72
    data table 73

representation and interpretation of
    data 73–4
  nature of science 71
  overview of 71
  puddle to pond activity 77–8
    permanent/temporary concept 76–7
  science understanding 71
  topic extension ideas 79
  visiting a pond 78–9
  watching puddles activity
    field trip 74
puppets, using 2

questioning 2, 3–4
  purposes of 3–4
  toolkit 4
quotition 160

reflection template 7
representations
  counting, multiple when 141–3
research skills 40
robotics 22–3
role-play
  exploration through 97
  reinforce learning by 96
  representation and communication by
    39, 83–4, 91–2

sand pit 126, 190–1
school
  first day 1–2
  location 3
  surroundings 3
school-based events 2–3
science
  arguments for/against teaching in early
    years 28–9
  attitude of teacher to 28
  biological *see* biological science
  checklists 5
  chemical *see* chemical science
  content areas 26

EARTH AND SPACE SCIENCE   223

early years, overview 25–6
earth and space *see* earth and space
    science
effective teaching 28
manipulating context 45
methods of teaching 29–30
nature of 27
physical *see* physical science
problem-solving as a team 45
resources for 30
scientific literacy 27
simulations, use of 21–2
skills *see* science skills
what constitutes 26
science skills
    asking questions 33, 99
    classify and explain 93
    classifying, using reason to 35–6, 83, 92
    collect and classify 98
    collect and record 44, 58, 67
    data gathering 44, 72–3, 88
    digital technologies, use of 48, 102–6
    drawing and labelling 49
    experience and observe 62–3
    experiment and observe 43, 47, 56, 58,
        88
    explore, observe and collect 37, 48
    forms of data representation 73
    hypothesise 99
    interpreting data 73
    manipulating materials 72, 84–6, 108
    observing 38, 55, 67, 80, 99
    observing and comparing 35, 38, 67, 106
    predictions, making 33, 37, 45, 47–8, 54,
        72, 88, 102, 108
    presentation of information 40
    record information 37, 44
    representing ideas 33, 93
    research 40
    responding to questions 32–3, 56, 72, 81,
        93, 99
    role-play to represent 39, 83–4, 91–2,
        96–7

scientific vocabulary, development 33,
    45, 56, 64, 81
testing ideas 108
scientific literacy 27
    diagrams, use of 33
    drawing and labelling 49
    organising observations 33
    re-representing forms of data 73
    science knowledge, decisions based on
        108
    symbols, use of 93
    tables and graphs, use of 44, 72–3, 101
    terminology, development of 45, 56, 84
self-assessment 6
shapes
    classroom discussion, learning 130
    play-based learning 127
    shape walk 188
    three-dimensional shapes
        making 186
        properties of 187
    two-dimensional shapes 181
        coathanger mobiles activity 184
        flips (reflection) 185
        pattern blocks , activities 182
        shape families 183
        slides (translation) 185
        symmetry 186
        tessellating shapes 184–5
        turns (rotations) 185
    vocabulary 130
simulations 21–2
skip counting 143
    100s and 1000s, in 145–6
    tens, in 144–5
    twos, in 145
statistics and probability
    chance concepts 173
        certain and impossible events 174
        two-outcome spinner 174
    data
        collection activities 176
        integration into–

statistics and probability (*continued*)
  integration into– (*continued*)
    biological science 31
    chemical science 53
    earth and space science 71
    physical science 91
strategies approach
  addition facts to 165–9
    bridging ten 168
    counting-on 166–7
    doubles and adding 10 167
    near doubles 169
    tens facts 167
  multiplication facts 170–1
    easy facts 170–1
    number grid 171
  number families 170
  subtraction facts 169–70
subitising 143
subtraction 154
  basic facts, learning 169–70
  problem types, presentation of 155
symbols, use of 93
  info-graphics 188

tables and graphs, use of 44, 72–3, 101
tablet devices, use of 19, 23
teacher-directed activities 3
teacher(s)
  connecting–
    different learning areas 209
    in- and out-of school experiences 209
  questioning 3–4
  reflection template 7
  role 2
teaching
  constructivist approach 2
  maths, styles–
    connectionist 125
    discovery 125
    transmission 125
  strategies 2–3
    addition basic facts, to 165–9

subtraction facts, to 169–70
technological pedagogical and content
    knowledge (TPACK) 15
terminology, development of 45, 56, 84
tests
  disguising 5–6
time 189, 195
  calendar 198–204
    creating 199
    daily routines, investigating 203–4
    days of the week 202–4
    months, exploration of 198–9
    representations of data 201
    seasons 200, 202
  IWB and ICT skills, use of 198–9
  lengths of, investigating 206
  relative times, concept of 207
  stories, chronological order 207
  teaching sequence 198
  telling the time 204–6
    apps, use of 205
    IWB clock images 205
    matching activity 206
  time-related concepts 197–8, 204
  time lapse activities 208
two-dimensional shapes 181
  coathanger mobiles activity 184
  flips (reflection) 185
  pattern blocks , activities 182
  shape families 183
  slides (translation) 185
  symmetry 186
  tessellating shapes 184–5
  turns (rotations) 185

Vallely, Dan
  The Great Possum Creek Bush Fire 38
video technology 117
  production 23, 83, 96, 117
  watching 10, 16, 39, 53, 55, 117
vocabulary development 31, 33, 48, 64, 96,
    100, 112
  class discussion, learning through 130

science terminology, development of 45, 56, 84
VoiceThread 119
volume
  concept development activities 189

weather, collection of data 178–9
wikis 119
wind study unit
  constructions using the wind 86–9
  drying clothes experiment 88–9
  explanation and nature of wind 80–4
    Beaufort Scale 81

classifying activity 83
digital weather stations 82
role-play 82
making air move 84–5
nature of science 80
overview of unit 80
science understanding 80
topic extension ideas 89
word wall 44, 96
wordle 33, 91, 96, 112–13
written responses
  assessment of 5
  reflection on 5